AAT

Qualifications and Credit Framework (QCF)
LEVEL 2 CERTIFICATE IN ACCOUNTING
(QCF)

QUESTION BANK

Basic Accounting II

2012 Edition

First edition 2010
Third edition June 2012

ISBN 9781 4453 9484 8 (previous edition 9780 7517 9757 2)

British Library Cataloguing-in-Publication Data
A catalogue record for this book is available from the British Library

Published by

BPP Learning Media Ltd
BPP House
Aldine Place
London W12 8AA

www.bpp.com/learningmedia

Printed in the United Kingdom

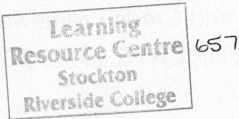

BPP
LEARNING MEDIA

CONTENTS

Introduction   v

Question and answer bank

A NOTE ABOUT COPYRIGHT

Dear Customer

What does the little © mean and why does it matter?

Your market-leading BPP books, course materials and e-learning materials do not write and update themselves. People write them: on their own behalf or as employees of an organisation that invests in this activity. Copyright law protects their livelihoods. It does so by creating rights over the use of the content.

Breach of copyright is a form of theft – as well as being a criminal offence in some jurisdictions, it is potentially a serious breach of professional ethics.

With current technology, things might seem a bit hazy but, basically, without the express permission of BPP Learning Media:

- Photocopying our materials is a breach of copyright

- Scanning, ripcasting or conversion of our digital materials into different file formats, uploading them to facebook or emailing them to your friends is a breach of copyright

You can, of course, sell your books, in the form in which you have bought them – once you have finished with them. (Is this fair to your fellow students? We update for a reason.)

And what about outside the UK? BPP Learning Media strives to make our materials available at prices students can afford by local printing arrangements, pricing policies and partnerships which are clearly listed on our website. A tiny minority ignore this and indulge in criminal activity by illegally photocopying our material or supporting organisations that do. If they act illegally and unethically in one area, can you really trust them?

INTRODUCTION

This is BPP Learning Media's AAT Question Bank for Basic Accounting II. It is part of a suite of ground-breaking resources produced by BPP Learning Media for the AAT's assessments under the qualification and credit framework.

The Basic Accounting II assessment is **computer assessed**. As well as being available in the traditional paper format, this **Question Bank is available in an online environment** containing tasks similar to those you will encounter in the AAT's testing environment. BPP Learning Media believe that the best way to practise for an online assessment is in an online environment. However, if you are unable to practise in the online environment you will find that all tasks in the paper Question Bank have been written in a style that is as close as possible to the style that you will be presented with in your online assessment.

This Question Bank has been written in conjunction with the BPP Text, and has been carefully designed to enable students to practise all of the learning outcomes and assessment criteria for the units that make up Basic Accounting II. It is fully up to date as at June 2012 and reflects both the AAT's unit guide and the practice assessments provided by the AAT.

This Question Bank contains these key features:

- tasks corresponding to each chapter of the Text. Some tasks are designed for learning purposes, others are of assessment standard

- the AAT's practice assessments and answers for Basic Accounting II and further BPP practice assessments

The emphasis in all tasks and assessments is on the practical application of the skills acquired.

VAT

You may find tasks throughout this Question Bank that need you to calculate or be aware of a rate of VAT. This is stated at 20% in these examples and questions.

Approaching the assessment

When you sit the assessment it is very important that you follow the on screen instructions. This means you need to carefully read the instructions, both on the introduction screens and during specific tasks.

When you access the assessment you should be presented with an introductory screen with information similar to that shown below (taken from the introductory screen from one of the AAT's practice assessments for Basic Accounting II).

This assessment is in TWO sections.
You must show competence in BOTH sections.
You should therefore attempt and aim to complete EVERY task in EACH section.
Each task is independent. You will not need to refer to your answers to previous tasks.
Read every task carefully to make sure you understand what is required.

Where the date is relevant, it is given in the task data.

Both minus signs and brackets can be used to indicate negative numbers UNLESS task instructions say otherwise.

You must use a full stop to indicate a decimal point.
For example, write 100.57 NOT 100,57 or 100 57

You may use a comma to indicate a number in the thousands, but you don't have to.
For example, 10000 and 10,000 are both OK.

Other indicators are not compatible with the computer-marked system.

Section 1 Complete all 6 tasks

Section 2 Complete all 8 tasks

The actual instructions will vary depending on the subject you are studying for. It is very important you read the instructions on the introductory screen and apply them in the assessment. You don't want to lose marks when you know the correct answer just because you have not entered it in the right format.

In general, the rules set out in the AAT practice assessments for the subject you are studying for will apply in the real assessment, but you should again read the information on this screen in the real assessment carefully just to make sure. This screen may also confirm the VAT rate used if applicable.

A full stop is needed to indicate a decimal point. We would recommend using minus signs to indicate negative numbers and leaving out the comma signs to indicate thousands, as this results in a lower number of key strokes and less margin for error when working under time pressure. Having said that, you can use whatever is easiest for you as long as you operate within the rules set out for your particular assessment.

You have to show competence in both sections of assessments and you should therefore complete all of the tasks. Don't leave questions unanswered.

In some assessments written or complex tasks may be human marked. In this case you are given a blank space or table to enter your answer into. You are told in the practice assessments which tasks these are (note: there may be none if all answers are marked by the computer).

If these involve calculations, it is a good idea to decide in advance how you are going to lay out your answers to such tasks by practising answering them on a word document, and certainly you should try all such tasks in this Question Bank and in the AAT's environment using the practice assessments.

When asked to fill in tables, or gaps, never leave any blank even if you are unsure of the answer. Fill in your best estimate.

Note that for some assessments where there is a lot of scenario information or tables of data provided (eg tax tables), you may need to access these via 'pop-ups'. Instructions will be provided on how you can bring up the necessary data during the assessment.

Finally, take note of any task specific instructions once you are in the assessment. For example, you may be asked to enter a date in a certain format or to enter a number to a certain number of decimal places.

Remember you can practise the BPP questions in this Question Bank in an online environment on our dedicated AAT Online page. On the same page is a link to the current AAT practice assessments as well.

If you have any comments about this book, please e-mail paulsutcliffe@bpp.com or write to Paul Sutcliffe, Senior Publishing Manager, BPP Learning Media Ltd, BPP House, Aldine Place, London W12 8AA.

Question bank

Question bank

Basic Accounting II Question bank

Chapter 1

Task 1.1

Natural Productions has a petty cash system based on an imprest amount of £100 which is replenished weekly. On Friday 20 January the total of the vouchers in the petty cash box was £68.34.

How much cash is required to replenish the petty cash box?

£

....

Task 1.2

Newmans, the music shop, has an imprest petty cash system based upon an imprest amount of £120.00. During the week ending 27 January the petty cash vouchers given below were presented, authorised and paid.

PETTY CASH VOUCHER		
Number: 0721		Date: 23 Jan
Details		Amount
Coffee		3 - 99
	Net	3 - 99
	VAT	-
	Gross	3 - 99
Claimed by:	T. Richards	
Authorised by:	J. Clarke	

PETTY CASH VOUCHER		
Number: 0726		Date: 27 Jan
Details		Amount
Computer disks		9 - 35
	Net	9 - 35
	VAT	1 - 87
	Gross	11 - 22
Claimed by:	D. Player	
Authorised by:	J. Clarke	

PETTY CASH VOUCHER

Number: 0722   Date: 23 Jan

Details		Amount
10 Books Postage Stamps		24 - 00
	Net	24 - 00
	VAT	-
	Gross	24 - 00

Claimed by: D. Player

Authorised by: J. Clarke

PETTY CASH VOUCHER

Number: 0723   Date: 24 Jan

Details		Amount
Taxi fare		8 - 94
	Net	8 - 94
	VAT	1 - 78
	Gross	10 - 72

Claimed by: P. L. Newman

Authorised by: J. Clarke

PETTY CASH VOUCHER

Number: 0724   Date: 24 Jan

Details		Amount
Printer paper		2 - 99
Envelopes		2 - 95
	Net	5 - 94
	VAT	1 - 18
	Gross	7 - 12

Claimed by: T. Richards

Authorised by: J. Clarke

PETTY CASH VOUCHER

Number: *0725*

Date: *26 Jan*

Details		Amount
Train fare		*13 - 60*
	Net	*13 - 60*
	VAT	*-*
	Gross	*13 - 60*

Claimed by: *P. L. Newman*

Authorised by: *J. Clarke*

You are required to:

(a) **Write up the petty cash vouchers in the petty cash book**

(b) **Total the petty cash book (credit side) and check that it cross-casts**

Petty cash book

Debit side			Credit side								
Date	Details	Amount £	Date	Details	Voucher number	Total £	VAT £	Travel £	Post £	Stationery £	Office supplies £
22 Jan	Bal b/f	120.00									

Cross-cast check:

	£
Office supplies	
Stationery	
Postage	
Travel	
VAT	
Total	

Task 1.3

On the first day of every month cash is drawn from the bank to restore the petty cash imprest level to £75.

A summary of petty cash transactions during November is shown below:

Opening balance on 1 November	£22
Cash from bank on 1 November	£53
Expenditure during month	£16

(a) **What will be the amount required to restore the imprest level on 1 December?**

£ [   ]

(b) **Will the receipt from the bank on 1 December be a debit or credit entry in the petty cash book?**

	✓
Debit	
Credit	

Task 1.4

Short Furniture has a monthly petty cash imprest system based upon an imprest amount of £150.00. During the month of January the following petty cash vouchers were authorised and paid:

Voucher No.	£
0473	12.60
0474	15.00
0475	19.75
0476	9.65
0477	10.00
0478	13.84
0479	4.26
0480	16.40

The cash in the petty cash box at 31 January was made up as follows:

£10 note	1
£5 note	4
£2 coin	3
£1 coin	7
50p coin	5
20p coin	8
10p coin	9
5p coin	4
2p coin	11
1p coin	8

(a) **Add together the voucher total and the petty cash in the box to arrive at the imprest amount at the end of January.**

	£
Voucher total	
Petty cash in the box	
Imprest amount	

(b) **The petty cash control account in the general ledger is given below. You are to balance the petty cash control account (this should be the same as the balance of cash in the petty cash box on 31 January).**

Petty cash control

		£			£
1 Jan	Balance b/f	150.00	31 Jan	Expenditure	101.50

Task 1.5

A business which is not registered for VAT has partially completed its petty cash book for November, as shown below.

Petty cash book

Debit side			Credit side					
Date	Details	Amount £	Date	Details	Total £	Stationery £	Postage £	Motor fuel £
1 Nov	Bal b/f	100	7 Nov	Postage stamps	20			
			15 Nov	Pens & pencils	18			
			22 Nov	Petrol	10			
			30 Nov	Envelopes	15			
	Total			Total				

(a) Complete the analysis columns for the four items purchased from petty cash.

(b) Total and balance the petty cash book, showing clearly the balance carried down at 30 November.

(c) Enter the balance brought down at 1 December, showing clearly the date, details, and amount. You do NOT need to restore the imprest amount.

....

Task 1.6

This is a summary of petty cash payments made by your business.

Post Office paid	£30.00 (no VAT)
Window cleaning paid	£25.60 plus VAT
MegaBus Company paid	£29.50 (no VAT)

(a) Enter the above transactions in the petty cash book.

(b) Total the petty cash book and show the balance carried down.

Petty cash book

Debit side		Credit side					
Details	Amount £	Details	Amount £	VAT £	Postage £	Travel £	Cleaning £
Balance b/f	175.00						

....

Task 1.7

Your business has paid two amounts from petty cash in the second week of September:

- Cleaning materials for £31.80 including VAT
- Courier costs for £51.75 plus VAT

(a) **Complete the petty cash vouchers below.**

Petty cash voucher		
Date: 13.9.XX		
Number: PC331		
Cleaning materials		
Net	£	
VAT	£	
Gross	£	

Petty cash voucher		
Date: 13.9.XX		
Number: PC332		
Courier costs		
Net	£	
VAT	£	
Gross	£	

By 20 September the petty cash control account has a balance of £96.70. The cash in the petty cash box is checked and the following notes and coins are there.

Notes and coins	£
2 × £20 notes	40.00
3 × £10 notes	30.00
2 × £5 notes	10.00
1 × £2 coins	2.00
5 × £1 coins	5.00
7 × 50p coins	3.50
11 × 10p coins	1.10
2 × 5p coins	0.10

(b) **Reconcile the cash amount in the petty cash box with the balance on the petty cash control account.**

Amount in petty cash box	£	
Balance on petty cash control account	£	
Difference	£	

At the end of September the cash in the petty cash box was £9.76.

(c) **Complete the petty cash reimbursement document below to restore the imprest amount of £250.**

Petty cash reimbursement		
Date: 30.09.20XX		
Amount required to restore the cash in the petty cash box	£	

Task 1.8

This is a summary of petty cash payments made by Kitchen Kuts.

Tom's Taxi paid	£18.00 (no VAT)
Post Office paid	£30.00 (no VAT)
SMP Stationery paid	£36.00 plus VAT

(a) **Enter the above transactions, in the order in which they are shown, in the petty cash book below.**

(b) **Total the petty cash book and show the balance carried down.**

Petty cash book

Debit side		Credit side					
Details	Amount £	Details	Amount £	VAT £	Postage £	Travel £	Stationery £
Balance b/f	150.00						

Task 1.9

Two amounts have been paid from petty cash:

- Envelopes for £16.80 including VAT
- Motor fuel for £32.00 plus VAT

(a) **Complete the petty cash vouchers below.**

Petty cash voucher		
Date: 7.07.XX		
Number: PC187		
5 packs A4 envelopes		
Net	£	
VAT	£	
Gross	£	

Petty cash voucher		
Date: 7.07.XX		
Number: PC188		
Fuel for motor van		
Net	£	
VAT	£	
Gross	£	

Part way through the month the petty cash control account had a balance of £120.00. The cash in the petty cash box was checked and the following notes and coins were there.

Notes and coins	£
3 × £20 notes	60.00
5 × £5 notes	25.00
17 × £1 coins	17.00
23 × 50p coins	11.50
16 × 10p coins	1.60
21 × 5p coins	1.05

(b) **Reconcile the cash amount in the petty cash box with the balance on the petty cash control account.**

Amount in petty cash box	£	
Balance on petty cash control account	£	
Difference	£	

At the end of the month the cash in the petty cash box was £3.45.

(c) **Complete the petty cash reimbursement document below to restore the imprest amount of £200.**

Petty cash reimbursement		
Date: 31.07.20XX		
Amount required to restore the cash in the petty cash box	£	

Chapter 2

Task 2.1

Given below is a completed cheque.

Who is the drawee?	
Who is the payee?	
Who is the drawer?	

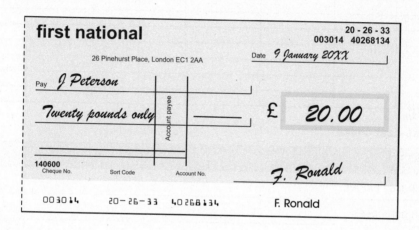

first national

20 - 26 - 33
003014 40268134

26 Pinehurst Place, London EC1 2AA

Date 9 January 20XX

Pay J Peterson

Twenty pounds only

£ 20.00

140600
Cheque No.   Sort Code   Account No.

F. Ronald

003014   20−26−33   40268134   F. Ronald

Task 2.2

You work for Natural Productions and one of your duties is to write up the cash book. Most of the payments are to credit suppliers but there are some purchases of materials (which all include VAT) from small suppliers with which Natural Productions does not have a credit account.

The cheque payment listing for the week ending 14 July is given below:

Cheque Payment Listing				
Date	Cheque number	Supplier	Amount £	Discount £
10 Jul	002156	W J Jones	521.36	10.50
10 Jul	002157	Cash purchase	415.80	
11 Jul	002158	Trenter Ltd	358.65	
11 Jul	002159	Packing Supplies	754.36	26.30
11 Jul	002160	Cash purchase	85.80	
12 Jul	002161	P J Phillips	231.98	
13 Jul	002162	O & P Ltd	721.30	17.56
14 Jul	002163	Cash purchase	107.52	

You are required to:

(a) Record these payments in the analysed cash book (credit side) given below

(b) Total the cash book (credit side) and check that it cross-casts

Cash book – credit side

Date	Details	Cheque no	Discounts received £	Bank £	VAT £	Cash purchases £	Purchases ledger £

Cross-cast check:

	£
Purchases ledger	
Cash purchases	
VAT	
Total	

Task 2.3

Given below are the cheque stubs for the six payments made by Newmans on 27 January.

You have also looked at the standing order and direct debit instruction file and noted that there is a standing order due to be paid to the local council for business rates of £255.00 on the 27th of each month, and a direct debit for rent of £500.00 also due on 27th of the month.

You are required to write up the cash book (credit side) given below, total it and check that it cross-casts.

Date 27 Jan 20XX

Henson Press

£ 329.00

003014

Date 27 Jan 20XX

Ely Instruments
Discount 12.80

£ 736.96

003015

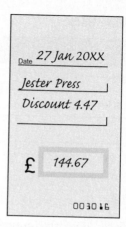

Date 27 Jan 20XX

Jester Press
Discount 4.47

£ 144.67

003016

Date 27 Jan 20XX

CD Supplies
Discount 1.96

£ 74.54

003017

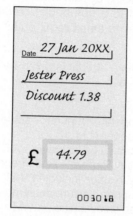

Date 27 Jan 20XX

Jester Press
Discount 1.38

£ 44.79

003018

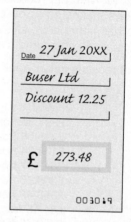

Date 27 Jan 20XX

Buser Ltd
Discount 12.25

£ 273.48

003019

Cash book – credit side

Date	Details	Cheque no	Discounts received £	Bank £	VAT £	Purchases ledger £	Rent & rates £

Cross-cast check:

	£
Rent & rates	
Purchases ledger	
Total	

Task 2.4

You work for Natural Productions. One of your duties is to write up the cash book. Natural Productions makes sales on credit to a number of credit customers who pay by cheque, and also has some cash sales from a small retail outlet attached to the factory for which customers pay in notes and coin.

The list of receipts in the week ending 14 July is given below.

RECEIPTS	
10 Jul	£891.36 from Superior Products – settlement discount £32.56
11 Jul	£295.68 from Hoppers Ltd
11 Jul	£138.24 from cash sales including VAT
13 Jul	£542.97 from Body Perfect – settlement discount £21.45
13 Jul	£209.76 from cash sales including VAT
14 Jul	£958.45 from Esporta Leisure settlement discount £42.58
14 Jul	£84.48 from cash sales including VAT
14 Jul	£752.45 from Langans Beauty

You are required to:

(a) **Record these receipts in the analysed cash book (debit side) given below**

(b) **Total the cash book (debit side) and check that it cross-casts**

Cash book – debit side

Date	Details	Discounts allowed £	Cash £	Bank £	VAT £	Cash sales £	Sales ledger £

Cross-cast check:

	£
Sales ledger	
Cash sales	
VAT	
Total	
Cash	
Bank	
Total	

Task 2.5

There are five payments to be entered in Canlan Ltd's cash book.

Receipts from suppliers for Canlan Ltd's cash purchases

Supplier: Dubai Dreams	**Supplier: Walter Enterprises**	**Supplier: Sinead Reilly**
Received cash with thanks for goods bought.	Received cash with thanks for goods bought.	Received cash with thanks for goods bought.
Net £270	Net £190	Net £56
VAT £54	VAT £38	(No VAT)
Total £324	Total £228	

Stubs from Canlan Ltd's cheque book

Payee: Sumatra Trading (Purchases ledger account PL026) £7,265 (Note: We have taken £35 settlement discount) Cheque number 093673	Payee: SHSK Co For stationery (Canlan Ltd has no credit account with this supplier) £378 including VAT Cheque number 093674

(a) **Enter the details of the three receipts from suppliers and two cheque book stubs into the credit side of the cash book shown below. Total each column.**

Cash book – credit side

Details	Discounts £	Cash £	Bank £	VAT £	Purchases ledger £	Cash purchases £	Stationery £
Balance b/f			236				
Dubai Dreams							
Walter Enterprises							
Sinead Reilly							
Sumatra Trading							
SHSK Co							
Total							

(b) There are two cheques from credit customers to be entered in the cash book:

Park Farm Stores   £2,576

Tristram Pale Ltd   £4,233 (this customer has taken a £25 discount)

Enter these details into the debit side of the cash book and total each column.

Cash book – debit side

Details	Discounts £	Cash £	Bank £	Sales ledger £
Balance b/f		1,228		
Park Farm Stores				
Tristram Pale Ltd				
Total				

(c) **Using your answers to (a) and (b) above, calculate the cash balance.**

£

(d) **Using your answers to (a) and (b) above, calculate the bank balance.**

£

(e) **Is the bank balance calculated in (d) above a debit or credit balance?**

	✓
Debit	
Credit	

Task 2.6

There are five payments to be entered in Kitchen Kuts' cash book.

Receipts

Received cash with thanks for goods bought. From Kitchen Kuts, a customer without a credit account. Net £200 VAT £40 Total £240 B. Smithson Ltd	Received cash with thanks for goods bought. From Kitchen Kuts, a customer without a credit account. Net £160 VAT £32 Total £192 H Hamnet	Received cash with thanks for goods bought. From Kitchen Kuts, a customer without a credit account. Net £320 (No VAT) Renee Reid

Cheque book counterfoils

Tenon Ltd (Purchase ledger account TEN006) £3,600 (Note: Have taken £80 settlement discount) 000168	Vernon Motor Repairs (We have no credit account with this supplier) £48 including VAT 000169

(a) **Enter the details from the three receipts and two cheque book stubs into the credit side of the cash book shown below and total each column.**

Cash book – credit side

Details	Discount £	Cash £	Bank £	VAT £	Purchases ledger £	Cash purchases £	Motor expenses £
Balance b/f			16,942				
B Smithson Ltd							
H Hamnet							
Renee Reid							
Tenon Ltd							
Vernon Motor Repairs							
Total							

There are two cheques from credit customers to be entered in Kitchen Kuts' cash book:

G Brownlow   £749

S Barnett   £300 (this customer has taken a £30 discount)

(b) **Enter the above details into the debit side of the cash book and total each column.**

Cash book – debit side

Details	Discount £	Cash £	Bank £	Sales ledger £
Balance b/f		1,325		
G Brownlow				
S Barnett				
Total				

(c) **Using your answers to (a) and (b) above, calculate the cash balance.**

£

(d) **Using your answers to (a) and (b) above, calculate the bank balance.**

£

(e) **Will the bank balance calculated in (d) above be a debit or credit balance?**

	✓
Debit	
Credit	

Chapter 3

Task 3.1

Would each of the following transactions appear as a debit or a credit on a business's bank statement?

Transaction	Debit ✓	Credit ✓
£470.47 paid into the bank		
Standing order of £26.79		
Cheque payment of £157.48		
Interest earned on the bank balance		
BACS payment for wages		

Task 3.2

You are given information about Newmans' receipts during the week ending 27 January. They represent payments by both credit customers and receipts for sales to non-credit customers of music, instruments and CDs which were settled by cheque.

From Tunfield District Council – £594.69

From Tunshire County Orchestra £468.29 – discount taken of £14.48

Sales of music (no VAT) – paid by cheque £478.90

From Tunfield Brass Band £1,059.72 – discount taken of £33.03

Sales of instruments (including VAT) – paid by cheque £752.16

Sales of CDs (including VAT) – paid by cheque £256.80

BPP LEARNING MEDIA

Write up and total the debit side of the cash book given below:

Cash book – debit side

Date	Details	Discounts allowed £	Bank £	VAT £	Sales ledger £	Music sales £	Instrument sales £	CD sales £	Interest £
	Bal b/f		379.22						

Task 3.3

Given below is the credit side of the cash book for Newmans for the week ending 27 January.

Cash book – credit side

Date	Cheque no	Details	Discounts received £	Bank £	VAT £	Purchases ledger £	Rent and rates £	Sundry £
27 Jan	003014	Henson Press		329.00		329.00		
27 Jan	003015	Ely Instr	12.80	736.96		736.96		
27 Jan	003016	Jester Press	4.47	144.67		144.67		
27 Jan	003017	CD Supplies	1.96	74.54		74.54		
27 Jan	003018	Jester Press	1.38	44.79		44.79		
27 Jan	003019	Buser Ltd	12.25	273.48		273.48		
27 Jan	SO	Rates		255.00			255.00	
27 Jan	DD	Rent		500.00			500.00	

Given below is the bank statement for Newmans for the week ending 27 January.

STATEMENT

first national
26 Pinehurst Place
London
EC1 2AA

NEWMANS

Account number: 20-26-33 40268134

CHEQUE ACCOUNT

Sheet 023

Date		Paid out	Paid in	Balance
20XX				
20 Jan	Balance b/f			379.22 CR
24 Jan	BGC - Tunsfield		594.69	
	BGC - Tunshire Co.		468.29	
24 Jan	SO - British Elec	212.00		1,230.20 CR
25 Jan	BGC - Tunsfield AOS		108.51	1,338.71 CR
26 Jan	Cheque No 003014	329.00		
	Credit		478.90	1,488.61 CR
27 Jan	Cheque No 003017	74.54		
	Cheque No 003015	736.96		
	Credit		1,059.72	
	Credit		752.16	
	SO - TDC	255.00		
	DD - Halpern Properties	500.00		
	Bank interest		3.68	1,737.67 CR

Compare the two sides of the cash book from Tasks 3.2 and 3.3 to the bank statement. Note any unmatched items below and state what action you would take.

Unmatched item	Action to be taken

Task 3.4

Amend both sides of the cash book and find the balance on the cash book at 27 January.

Cash book – debit side

Date	Details	Discounts allowed £	Bank £	VAT £	Sales ledger £	Music sales £	Instrument sales £	CD sales £	Interest £
	Balance b/f		379.22						
27 Jan	Tunfield DC		594.69✓		594.69				
27 Jan	Tunshire CO	14.48	468.29✓		468.29				
27 Jan	Non-credit sales		478.90✓			478.90			
27 Jan	Tunfield BB	33.03	1,059.72✓		1,059.72				
27 Jan	Non-credit sales		752.16✓	125.36			626.80		
27 Jan	Non-credit sales		256.80	42.80				214.00	

Cash book – credit side

Date	Cheque no.	Details	Discounts received £	Bank £	VAT £	Purchases ledger £	Rent & rates £	Sun £
27 Jan	003014	Henson Press		329.00✓		329.00		
27 Jan	003015	Ely Instr	12.80	736.96✓		736.96		
27 Jan	003016	Jester Press	4.47	144.67		144.67		
27 Jan	003017	CD Supplies	1.96	74.54✓		74.54		
27 Jan	003018	Jester Press	1.38	44.79		44.79		
27 Jan	003019	Buser Ltd	12.25	273.48		273.48		
27 Jan	SO	Rates		255.00✓			255.00	
27 Jan	DD	Rent		500.00✓			500.00	

Task 3.5

Prepare the bank reconciliation statement as at 27 January.

Bank reconciliation statement as at 27 January

	£	£
Balance per bank statement		
Outstanding lodgement		
Total to add		
Unpresented cheques		
Total to subtract		
Amended cash book balance		

Task 3.6

On 28 November The Flower Chain received the following bank statement as at 25 November:

High Street Bank plc The Concourse, Badley, B72 5DG				
To: The Flower Chain	Account no:	28710191		Date: 25 November

Statement of Account

Date	Details	Paid out £	Paid in £	Balance £
03 Nov	Balance b/f			9,136 C
07 Nov	Cheque 110870	6,250		2,886 C
17 Nov	Cheque 110872	2,250		636 C
21 Nov	Cheque 110865	3,670		3,034 D
	Direct Debit			
	– Insurance Ensured	500		3,534 D
21 Nov	Bank Giro Credit			
	– BBT Ltd		10,000	6,466 C
24 Nov	Bank Giro Credit			
	– Petals Ltd		2,555	9,021 C
	Direct Debit			
	– Rainbow Ltd	88		8,933 C
25 Nov	Cheque 110871	1,164		7,769 C

D = Debit C = Credit

The cash book as at 28 November is shown below.

Cash book

Date	Details	Bank £	Date	Cheque no.	Details	Bank £
01 Nov	Balance b/f	5,466	03 Nov	110870	Roberts & Co	6,250
24 Nov	Bevan & Co	1,822	03 Nov	110871	J Jones	1,164
24 Nov	Plant Pots Ltd	7,998	06 Nov	110872	Lake Walks Ltd	2,250
			10 Nov	110873	PH Supplies	275
			17 Nov	110874	Peters & Co	76

(a) Check the items on the bank statement against the items in the cash book.

(b) Update the cash book as needed.

(c) Total the cash book and clearly show the balance carried down at 28 November AND brought down at 29 November.

(d) Using the information from the cash book and bank statement, prepare a bank reconciliation statement as at 28 November.

Bank reconciliation statement as at 28 November

	£
Balance per bank statement:	
Add:	
Name:	
Name:	
Total to add	
Less:	
Name:	
Name:	
Total to subtract	
Balance as per cash book	

Task 3.7

(a) Which TWO of the following items reconciling the cash book to the bank statement are referred to as timing differences?

	Timing difference? ✓
Bank charges not recorded in the cash book	
Outstanding lodgements	
Interest charged not recorded in the cash book	
Unpresented cheques	

(b) Your cash book at 31 December shows a bank balance of £565 overdrawn. On comparing this with your bank statement at the same date, you discover the following:

A cheque for £57 drawn by you on 29 December has not yet been presented for payment.

A cheque for £92 from a customer, which was paid into the bank on 24 December, has been dishonoured on 31 December.

The correct bank balance at 31 December is:

	✓
£714 overdrawn	
£657 overdrawn	
£473 overdrawn	
£530 overdrawn	

(c) The cash book shows a bank balance of £5,675 overdrawn at 31 August. It is subsequently discovered that a standing order for £125 has been entered in the cash book twice, and that a dishonoured cheque for £450 has been debited in the cash book instead of credited.

The correct bank balance should be:

	✓
£5,100 overdrawn	
£6,000 overdrawn	
£6,250 overdrawn	
£6,450 overdrawn	

(d) Your firm's cash book at 30 April shows a balance at the bank of £2,490. Comparison with the bank statement at the same date reveals the following differences:

	£
Unpresented cheques	840
Bank charges	50
Receipts not yet credited by the bank	470
Dishonoured cheque from customer not in cash book	140

The correct balance on the cash book at 30 April is:

	✓
£1,460	
£2,300	
£2,580	
£3,140	

(e) The bank statement at 31 December 20X1 shows a balance of £1,000. The cash book shows a balance of £750.

Which of the following is the most likely reason for the difference?

	✓
Receipts of £250 recorded in cash book, but not yet recorded by bank	
Bank charges of £250 shown on the bank statement, not in the cash book	
Standing orders of £250 included on bank statement, not in the cash book	
Cheques issued for £250 recorded in the cash book, but not yet gone through the bank account	

(f) Your firm's cash book at 30 April shows a balance at the bank of £3,526. Comparison with the bank statement at the same date reveals the following differences:

	£
Unpresented cheques	920
Bank interest received not in cash book	150
Uncredited lodgements	270
Dishonour of customer's cheque not in cash book	310

The correct cash book balance at 30 April is:

£ [   ]

Task 3.8

On 26 July Ottaways Ltd received the following bank statement from Ronda Bank as at 23 July.

Assume today's date is 28 July.

Ronda Bank PLC

Bank Buildings, Flitweck, FT87 1XQ

To: Ottaways Ltd　　　　　Account No 56235472　　　23 July 20XX

Statement of Account

Date	Detail	Paid out	Paid in	Balance	
20XX		£	£	£	
03 Jul	Balance b/f			1,855	C
03 Jul	Cheque 126459	3,283		1,428	D
03 Jul	Cheque 126460	1,209		2,637	D
03 Jul	Cheque 126461	4,221		6,858	D
04 Jul	Cheque 126464	658		7,516	D
09 Jul	Bank Giro Credit SnipSnap Co		8,845	1,329	C
11 Jul	Cheque 126462	1,117		212	C
11 Jul	Direct Debit Flit DC	500		288	D
18 Jul	Direct Debit Consol Landlords	475		763	D
20 Jul	Bank Charges	32		795	D
22 Jul	Interest for month	103		898	D
23 Jul	Paid in at Ronda Bank		5,483	4,585	C

D = Debit   C = Credit

The cash book as at 23 July is shown below.

(a) **Check the items on the bank statement against the items in the cash book.**

(b) **Using the picklist below for the details column, enter any items in the cash book as needed.**

(c) **Total the cash book and clearly show the balance carried down at 23 July and brought down at 24 July.**

(d) **Using the picklist below, complete the bank reconciliation statement as at 23 July.**

Cash book

Date 20XX	Details	Bank £	Date 20XX	Cheque number	Details	Bank £
01 Jul	Balance b/f	1,855	01 Jul	126459	Gumpley Co	3,283
20 Jul	Brimfull Ltd	5,483	01 Jul	126460	Warnes Ltd	1,209
21 Jul	Adera Ltd	2,198	01 Jul	126461	Veldt Partners	4,221
22 Jul	Mist Northern	1,004	01 Jul	126462	Pathways	1,117
		▼	02 Jul	126463	Lindstrom Co	846
			02 Jul	126464	Kestrels Training	658
			13 Jul	126465	HGW Ltd	3,200
			13 Jul		Flit DC	500
					▼	
					▼	
					▼	
					▼	
	▼					

Bank reconciliation statement as at 23 July 20XX

Balance per bank statement		£	
Add outstanding lodgements:			
Name:	▼	£	
Name:	▼	£	
Total to add		£	
Less unpresented cheques:			
Name:	▼	£	
Name:	▼	£	
Total to subtract		£	
Balance as per cash book		£	

Picklist for line items:

Pathways
Flit DC
Balance b/d
Balance c/d
Bank charges
SnipSnap Co
Mist Northern
Interest
Gumpley Co
Lindstrom Co
Kestrels Training
Adera Ltd
Veldt Partners
Warnes Ltd
HGW Ltd
Brimfull Ltd
Consol Landlords

....

Chapter 4

Task 4.1

Your organisation is not registered for VAT. The balance on the sales ledger control account on 1 January was £11,689. The transactions that take place during January are summarised below:

	£
Credit sales	12,758
Sales returns	1,582
Cash received from trade receivables	11,563
Discounts allowed to trade receivables	738
Irrecoverable debt to be written off	389
Dishonoured cheque from customer	722

You are required to write up the sales ledger control account for the month of January.

Sales ledger control

	£		£

Task 4.2

Your organisation is not registered for VAT. The opening balance on the purchases ledger control account at 1 January was £8,347. The transactions for the month of January have been summarised below:

	£
Credit purchases	9,203
Purchases returns	728
Payments to trade payables	8,837
Discounts received	382

You are required to write up the purchases ledger control account for the month of January.

Purchases ledger control

	£		£

Task 4.3

This is a summary of transactions with credit suppliers during June.

	£
Balance of trade payables at 1 June	85,299
Goods bought on credit – gross	39,300
Payments made to credit suppliers	33,106
Discounts received	1,000
Goods returned to credit suppliers – gross	275

Prepare a purchases ledger control account from the details shown above. Show clearly the balance carried down at 30 June AND brought down at 1 July.

Purchases ledger control

Date	Details	Amount £	Date	Details	Amount £

Task 4.4

(a) The sales ledger control account at 1 May had a balance of £31,475. During May, gross sales of £125,000 were made on credit. Receipts from trade receivables amounted to £122,500 and settlement discounts of £550 were allowed. Credit notes of £1,300 gross were issued to customers.

The closing balance at 31 May is:

	✓
£32,125	
£33,975	
£34,725	
£33,225	

(b) Your purchases ledger control account has a balance at 1 October of £34,500 credit. During October, gross credit purchases were £78,400, gross cash purchases were £2,400 and payments made to suppliers, excluding cash purchases, and after deducting settlement discounts of £1,200, were £68,900. Gross purchases returns were £4,700.

The closing balance was:

	✓
£38,100	
£40,500	
£47,500	
£49,900	

Task 4.5

Assuming they all include VAT where relevant, identify the double entry for the following transactions.

	Bank £ DR/CR	SLCA £ DR/CR	PLCA £ DR/CR	VAT £ DR/CR	Purchases £ DR/CR	Sales returns £ DR/CR	Discounts received £ DR/CR	Discounts allowed £ DR/CR
Gross credit purchases £3,390								
Gross credit sales returns £1,860								
Payments to credit suppliers £4,590								
Receipts from credit customers £5,480								
Discounts allowed £400								
Discounts received £200								

Task 4.6

A credit customer, B B Brand Ltd, has ceased trading, owing Kitchen Kuts £1,560 plus VAT.

Record the journal entries needed in the general ledger to write off the net amount and the VAT.

Account name	Amount £	Debit ✓	Credit ✓

Chapter 5

Task 5.1

When reconciling sales ledger and purchases ledger control accounts to the list of balances from the subsidiary ledgers, would the following errors affect the relevant control account, the list of balances or both?

	Control account ✓	List of balances ✓	Both ✓
Invoice entered into the sales day book as £980 instead of £890			
Purchases day book overcast by £1,000			
Discounts allowed of £20 not entered into the cash book			
An invoice taken as £340 instead of £440 when being posted to the customer's account			
Incorrect balancing of a subsidiary ledger account			
A purchases return not entered into the purchases returns day book			

Task 5.2

James has just completed his first month of trading. James makes sales on credit to four customers and the transactions during his second month of trading were as follows:

Gross sales	£
To H Simms	2,000
To P Good	2,700
To K Mitchell	1,100
To C Brown	3,800

Receipts	£
From H Simms	2,400
From P Good	3,600
From K Mitchell	1,100
From C Brown	4,800

You are required to:

(a) **Show these transactions in total in the sales ledger control account and in detail in the individual sales ledger accounts. Each of the accounts shows, where appropriate, the opening balance at the start of the second month**

(b) **Balance the sales ledger control account and the individual sales ledger accounts**

(c) **Reconcile the list of sales ledger balances to the balance on the control account**

Sales ledger control

	£		£
Balance b/f	5,000		

Sales ledger

H Simms

	£		£
Balance b/f	900		

P Good

	£		£
Balance b/f	1,600		

K Mitchell

	£			£

C Brown

	£			£
Balance b/f	2,500			

Reconciliation of sales ledger balances with control account balance

	£
H Simms	
P Good	
K Mitchell	
C Brown	
Sales ledger control account	

Task 5.3

James also buys goods on credit from three suppliers. The transactions with these suppliers in month two are summarised below:

	£
Gross purchases:	
From J Peters	1,600
From T Sands	2,500
From L Farmer	3,200
Payments:	
To J Peters	1,700
To T Sands	3,200
To L Farmer	3,000

You are required to:

(a) **Show these transactions in total in the purchases ledger control account and in detail in the individual purchases ledger accounts given. Each of the accounts given shows the opening balance at the start of month two**

(b) **Balance the purchases ledger control account and the individual purchases ledger accounts**

(c) **Reconcile the list of purchases ledger balances to the balance on the control account**

Purchases ledger control

	£		£
		Balance b/f	2,700

Purchases ledger

J Peters

	£		£
		Balance b/f	300

T Sands

	£		£
		Balance b/f	1,700

L Farmer

	£		£
		Balance b/f	700

Reconciliation of purchases ledger balances with control account balance

	£
J Peters	
T Sands	
L Farmer	
Purchases ledger control account	

Task 5.4

The balance on a business's sales ledger control account at 30 June was £13,452. However the list of balances in the sales ledger totalled £12,614. The difference was investigated and the following errors were discovered:

(i)   The sales returns day book was undercast by £100.

(ii) A payment from one trade receivable had been correctly entered into the cash book as £350 but had been entered into the sales ledger as £530.

(iii) An irrecoverable debt of £200 had been written off in the sales ledger but had not been entered into the general ledger accounts.

(iv) A balance of £358 due from one trade receivable had been omitted from the list of sales ledger balances.

You are required to write up the corrected sales ledger control account and to reconcile this to the corrected list of sales ledger balances.

Sales ledger control

	£		£

	£
Sales ledger list of balances	
Error:	
Error:	
Amended list of balances	
Amended control account balance	

Task 5.5

The balance on an organisation's purchases ledger control account at 30 June was £26,677 whereas the total of the list of purchases ledger balances was £27,469. The following errors were discovered:

(i)   One total in the purchases day book had been undercast by £1,000.

(ii)   A discount received from a supplier of £64 had not been posted to his account in the purchases ledger.

(iii)   A debit balance of £120 had been included in the list of purchases ledger balances as a credit balance.

(iv)   Discounts received of £256 were credited to both the discounts received account and to the purchases ledger control account.

You are required to correct the purchases ledger control account and to reconcile the corrected balance to the corrected list of purchases ledger balances.

Purchases ledger control

	£		£

	£
Purchases ledger list of balances	
Error:	
Error:	
Error:	
Amended list of balances	
Amended control account balance	

Task 5.6

This is a summary of your business's transactions with credit customers during November.

	£
Balance of trade receivables at 1 November	48,125
Goods sold on credit (gross value)	37,008
Money received from credit customers	28,327
Discounts allowed	240
Goods returned by customers (gross value)	2,316

(a) **Prepare a sales ledger control account from the details shown above. Show clearly the balance carried down at 30 November AND brought down at 1 December.**

Sales ledger control

Date	Details	Amount £	Date	Details	Amount £

The following balances were in the sales ledger on 1 December:

	£
J Hicks Ltd	3,298
Parks and Gardens	4,109
Greener Grass	18,250
TTL Ltd	18,106
Reeves and Wright	10,400

(b) **Reconcile the balances shown above with the sales ledger control account balance you have calculated in part (a).**

	£
Sales ledger control account balance as at 1 December	
Total of sales ledger accounts as at 1 December	
Difference	

(c) **Because of an error in the sales ledger, there is a difference. What might have caused the difference? Tick TWO reasons only.**

	✓
VAT has been overstated on an invoice.	
VAT has been understated on an invoice.	
A sales invoice has been entered in the sales ledger twice.	
A sales credit note has been entered in the sales ledger twice.	
A receipt from a customer has been omitted from the sales ledger.	
A receipt from a customer has been entered in the sales ledger twice.	

Task 5.7

A business has the following transactions in one week.

	£
Credit purchases (at list price)	4,500
Sales on credit (at list price)	6,000
Purchase of a van (at list price)	10,460
Entertaining (no VAT)	360
Purchase of a car (no VAT)	8,600

A settlement discount of £300 is available on the sales. All figures are given exclusive of VAT at 20%.

If the balance on the VAT account was £2,165 credit at the beginning of the week, what is the balance at the end of the week?

£

Task 5.8

The following transactions take place during a three month period:

	£
Sales on credit including VAT at 20%	126,900.00
Purchases on credit including VAT	57,810.00
Credit notes issued including VAT	2,820.00
VAT incurred on cash expenses	271.50

The amount payable to HMRC for the quarter will be

£

BPP
LEARNING MEDIA

Task 5.9

At the end of the last VAT period, the VAT account for Fast Fashions showed that a refund was due from HM Revenue & Customs.

(a) **State ONE reason that would cause a refund to be due to Fast Fashions.**

Sales in June totalled £129,240 all including VAT

(b) **What is the amount of output VAT on sales?**

£	

Task 5.10

(a) A supplier sends you a statement showing a balance outstanding of £14,350. Your own records show a balance outstanding of £14,500.

The reason for this difference could be that

	✓
The supplier sent an invoice for £150 which you have not yet received	
The supplier has allowed you £150 settlement discount which you had not entered in your ledger	
You have paid the supplier £150 which he has not yet accounted for	
You have returned goods worth £150 which the supplier has not yet accounted for	

(b) An invoice for £69 has been recorded in the sales day book as £96.

When the sales ledger reconciliation is prepared, adjustments will be required to:

	✓
The control account only	
The list of balances only	
Both the control account and the list of balances	

(c) The total of the balances on the individual suppliers' accounts in Arnold's purchases ledger is £81,649. The balance on the purchases ledger control account is £76,961. He has discovered that an invoice for £4,688 has been posted twice to the correct supplier's account and that payments totalling £1,606 which he made by standing order have been omitted from his records.

The corrected balance for trade payables is

£

Task 5.11

(a) You have been handed an aged receivable analysis which shows a total balance of £109,456.

This amount should reconcile with which TWO of the following?

	✓
The balance on the bank statement	
The balance on the sales ledger control account	
The balance on the purchases ledger control account	
The total of all the purchases ledger balances	
The total of all the sales ledger balances	

(b) **Complete the following sentence:**

The aged receivable analysis shows:

	✓
How much is owed to suppliers at any point	
Over how many months the outstanding balance owed by each individual credit customer has built up	
The total purchases over the year to date to each credit supplier	

Chapter 6

Task 6.1

Peter Knight is one of the employees at Short Furniture and has a gross weekly wage of £440.00. For this week his income tax payable through the PAYE system is £77.76. The employees' NIC for the week is £43.18 and 5% of his gross wage is deducted each week as a pension contribution. The employer's NIC for the week is £49.35.

(a) **Calculate Peter's net wage for the week.**

£

(b) **What payments and to whom should Short Furniture make in regard to Peter's wages for this week?**

	should be paid to	
	should be paid to	
	should be paid to	

(c) **Show how all of the elements of Peter's weekly wage would be entered into the accounting records by writing up the ledger accounts given.**

Wages expense

	£		£

Wages control

	£		£

PAYE/NIC payable

	£		£

Pension payable

	£		£

Bank

	£		£

··

Task 6.2

An organisation has started a new business and a new set of accounts are to be opened. The opening balances for the new business are as follows:

	£
Capital	10,000
Furniture and fittings	15,315
Sales	127,318
Motor vehicles	20,109
Cash at bank	15,000
Purchases	86,120
Purchases returns	750
Purchases ledger control	37,238
Sales ledger control	53,259
Loan from bank	7,000
Motor expenses	1,213
VAT (owed to HMRC)	8,710

Prepare a journal to enter these opening balances into the accounts.

Journal

Account name	Debit £	Credit £
Totals		

....

Task 6.3

A credit customer, ABC Ltd, has ceased trading, owing your firm £240 plus VAT.

Prepare a journal to write off the net amount and VAT in the general ledger.

Journal

Account name	Amount £	Debit ✓	Credit ✓

....

Task 6.4

You have the following information for your business, First Fashions:

(a) £50 has been debited to the discounts received account instead of the discounts allowed account.

(b) A payment of £200 for office expenses has been credited to the bank deposit account instead of the bank current account.

(c) A credit customer, Kit & Company, has ceased trading, owing First Fashions £2,800 plus VAT. The net amount and VAT must be written off in the general ledger.

Record the journal entries needed in the general ledger to deal with this information.

Journal

Account names	Amount £	Debit ✓	Credit ✓

Task 6.5

A credit customer, Arco and Co, has ceased trading, owing your business £2,370 plus VAT.

Record the journal entries needed in the general ledger to write off the net amount and the VAT.

Account name	Amount £	Debit ✓	Credit ✓

Task 6.6

A new business has already started to trade, though it is not yet registered for VAT, and now wishes to open up its first set of accounts. You are handed the following information:

It has £1,000 in the bank, petty cash of £200 and trade receivables of £7,700. It owes the bank for a loan of £9,000 and started with cash from its owner of £500. It has made sales so far of £15,250 and purchases of £6,230, for which it still owes one supplier £3,400. Expenses paid to date have been £7,020, and a van was bought for cash of £6,000.

Record the journal entries needed in the accounts in the general ledger of the business to deal with the opening entries.

Account name	Amount £	Debit ✓	Credit ✓
Journal to record the opening entries of new business			

Task 6.7

Kitchen Kuts has started a new business, Kitchen Capers, and a new set of accounts is to be opened. A partially completed journal to record the opening entries is shown below.

Record the journal entries needed in the accounts in the general ledger of Kitchen Capers to deal with the opening entries.

Account name	Amount £	Debit ✓	Credit ✓
Cash	150		
Cash at bank	12,350		
Capital	23,456		
Fixtures and Fittings	2,100		
Insurance	825		
Loan from bank	10,000		
Miscellaneous expenses	218		
Motor vehicle	15,650		
Office expenses	613		
Rent and rates	1,550		
Journal to record the opening entries of new business			

Chapter 7

Task 7.1

A business extracts a trial balance in which the debit column totals £452,409 and the credit column totals £463,490.

What will be the balance on the suspense account?

Account name	Amount £	Debit ✓	Credit ✓
Suspense			

Task 7.2

A business used a suspense account with a credit balance of £124 to balance its initial trial balance.

Correction of which ONE of the following errors will clear the suspense account?

Error	✓
A credit note from a supplier with a net amount of £124 was not entered in the purchases ledger	
Discounts allowed of £124 were only posted to the discounts allowed account	
A cash purchase for £124 was not entered in the purchases account	
An irrecoverable debt write-off of £124 was not entered in the subsidiary ledger	

Task 7.3

Given below are two ledger accounts.

Examine them carefully and then re-write them correcting any errors that have been made (you may assume that the balance brought forward on the VAT account is correct).

Sales ledger control

	£		£
Sales	15,899	Balance b/f	1,683
Discounts allowed	900	Bank	14,228
Sales returns	1,467	Irrecoverable debts written off	245
		Balance c/d	2,110
	18,266		18,266

VAT

	£		£
Sales	2,368	Balance b/f	2,576
Purchase returns	115	Purchases	1,985
Balance c/d	2,078		
	4,561		18,266

Sales ledger control

Details	£	Details	£

VAT

Details	£	Details	£

Task 7.4

The trial balance of Harry Parker & Co has been prepared by the bookkeeper and the total of the debit balances is £427,365 while the total of the credit balances is £431,737. The difference was dealt with by setting up a suspense account and then the ledger accounts were investigated to try to find the causes of the difference. The following errors and omissions were found:

(i) The total of the sales day book was undercast by £1,000.

(ii) The balance on the electricity account of £1,642 had been completely omitted from the trial balance.

(iii) Discounts allowed of £865 had been entered on the wrong side of the discounts allowed account.

(iv) Receipts from trade receivables of £480 had been entered into the accounts as £840.

(v) A discount received of £120 had been completely omitted from the cash book.

You are required to:

(a) **Draft journal entries to correct each of these errors or omissions.**

Journal entries

			£	£
(i)	Debit			
	Credit			
(ii)	Debit			
	Credit			
(iii)	Debit			
	Credit			
	Debit			
	Credit			
(iv)	Debit			
	Credit			
(v)	Debit			
	Credit			

(b) **Write up the suspense account showing clearly the opening balance and how the suspense account is cleared after correction of each of the errors.**

Suspense

Details	£	Details	£

Task 7.5

After extracting an initial trial balance a business finds it has a debit balance of £118 in the suspense account. You have the following information.

(a) Sales of £500 have been credited to the sales returns account.

(b) Entries to record a bank payment of £125 for office expenses have been reversed.

(c) A bank payment of £299 for purchases (no VAT) has been entered correctly in the purchases column of the cash book but as £29 in the total Bank column.

(d) Discounts allowed of £388 were only posted to the sales ledger control account in the general ledger.

Record the journal entries needed in the general ledger to (i) reverse incorrect entries and (ii) record the transactions correctly.

The Journal

Account names	Debit £	Credit £
(a)		
(b)		
(c)		
(d)		

Task 7.6

On 30 June, a suspense account of a business that is not registered for VAT has a credit balance of £720.

On 1 July, the following errors were discovered:

- A bank payment of £225 has been omitted from the rent and rates account.

- An irrecoverable debt expense of £945 has been credited correctly to the sales ledger control account, but debited to both the irrecoverable debt account and the sales account.

(a) **Enter the opening balance in the suspense account below.**

(b) **Make the necessary entries to clear the suspense account.**

Suspense

Date	Details	Amount £	Date	Details	Amount £

Task 7.7

(a) When posting an invoice received for building maintenance, £980 was entered on the building maintenance expense account instead of the correct amount of £890.

What correction should be made to the building maintenance expenses account?

	✓
Debit £90	
Credit £90	
Debit £1,780	
Credit £1,780	

(b) A business receives an invoice from a supplier for £2,800 which is mislaid before any entry has been made, resulting in the transaction being omitted from the books entirely.

This is an

	✓
Error of transposition	
Error of omission	
Error of principle	
Error of commission	

(c) An error of commission is one where

	✓
A transaction has not been recorded	
One side of a transaction has been recorded in the wrong account, and that account is of a different class to the correct account	
One side of a transaction has been recorded in the wrong account, and that account is of the same class as the correct account	
A transaction has been recorded using the wrong amount	

(d) **Which ONE of the following is an error of principle?**

	✓
A gas bill credited to the gas account and debited to the bank account	
The purchase of a non-current asset credited to the asset account and debited to the supplier's account	
The purchase of a non-current asset debited to the purchases account and credited to the supplier's account	
The payment of wages debited and credited to the correct accounts, but using the wrong amount	

(e) Where a transaction is entered into the correct ledger accounts, but the wrong amount is used, the error is known as an error of

	✓
Omission	
Original entry	
Commission	
Principle	

(f) When a trial balance was prepared, two ledger accounts were omitted:

Discounts received	£6,150
Discounts allowed	£7,500

A suspense account was opened.

What was the balance on the suspense account?

	✓
Debit £1,350	
Credit £1,350	
Debit £13,650	
Credit £13,650	

(g) If a purchases return of £48 has been wrongly posted to the debit of the sales returns account, but has been correctly entered in the purchases ledger control account, the total of the trial balance would show

	✓
The credit side to be £48 more than the debit side	
The debit side to be £48 more than the credit side	
The credit side to be £96 more than the debit side	
The debit side to be £96 more than the credit side	

(h) **Indicate whether preparing a trial balance will reveal the following errors.**

	Yes	No
Omitting both entries for a transaction		
Posting the debit entry for an invoice to an incorrect expense account		
Omitting the debit entry for a transaction		
Posting the debit entry for a transaction as a credit entry		

Task 7.8

Show which of the errors below are, or are not, disclosed by the trial balance.

Error in the general ledger	Error disclosed by the trial balance ✓	Error NOT disclosed by the trial balance ✓
Recording a bank receipt of a cash sale on the debit side of the cash sales account		
Entering an insurance expense in the administration expenses account		
Entering the discounts received account balance on the debit side of the trial balance		
Miscasting the total column of one page of the sales returns day book		
Failing to write up a dishonoured cheque in the cash book		
Recording discount allowed of £15 as £150 in the cash book		

Task 7.9

Your organisation's trial balance included a suspense account. All the bookkeeping errors have now been traced and the journal entries shown below have been recorded.

Journal entries

Account name	Debit £	Credit £
Motor vehicles	4,300	
Machinery		4,300
Suspense	750	
Sales ledger control		750
Discounts allowed	209	
Suspense		209

Post the journal entries to the general ledger accounts Dates are not required but you must complete the 'details' columns accurately.

Discounts allowed

Details	Amount £	Details	Amount £

Machinery

Details	Amount £	Details	Amount £

Motor vehicles

Details	Amount £	Details	Amount £

Sales ledger control

Details	Amount £	Details	Amount £

Suspense

Details	Amount £	Details	Amount £
		Balance b/f	541

Task 7.10

Your business extracted an initial trial balance which did not balance, and a suspense account was opened. Journal entries were subsequently prepared to correct the errors that had been found, and clear the suspense account. The list of balances in the initial trial balance, and the journal entries to correct the errors, are shown below. The balances do not yet reflect the journal entries.

Taking into account the journal entries, which will clear the suspense account, redraft the trial balance by placing the figures in the debit or credit column.

	Balances extracted on 30 June £	Balances at 1 July	
		Debit £	Credit £
Machinery	82,885		
Computer equipment	41,640		
Insurance	17,520		
Bank overdraft	13,252		
Petty cash	240		
Sales ledger control	241,500		
Purchases ledger control	134,686		
VAT owing to HM Revenue and Customs	19,920		
Capital	44,826		
Sales	525,092		
Purchases	269,400		
Purchases returns	16,272		
Wages	61,680		
Maintenance expenses	3,283		
Stationery	8,049		
Rent and rates	3,466		
Heat and light	5,172		
Telephone	7,596		
Marketing expenses	5,327		
Suspense (debit balance)	6,290		
Totals			

Journal entries

Account name	Debit £	Credit £
Sales ledger control	2,875	
Suspense		2,875
Sales ledger control	2,875	
Suspense		2,875

Account name	Debit £	Credit £
Heat and light		5,172
Suspense	5,172	
Heat and light	5,712	
Suspense		5,712

Task 7.11

Kitchen Kuts' initial trial balance includes a suspense account with a balance of £100.

The error has been traced to the sales returns day book shown below.

Sales returns day book

Date 20XX	Details	Credit note number	Total £	VAT £	Net £
30 June	Barber Bates Ltd	367	720	120	600
30 June	GTK Ltd	368	4,320	720	3,600
30 June	Peer Prints	369	960	160	800
	Totals		6,000	1,100	5,000

(a) **Identify the error and record the journal entries needed in the general ledger to**

(i) **Remove the incorrect entry**

Account name	Amount £	Debit ✓	Credit ✓

(ii) **Record the correct entry**

Account name	Amount £	Debit ✓	Credit ✓

(iii) **Remove the suspense account balance**

Account name	Amount £	Debit ✓	Credit ✓

An entry to record a bank payment of £350 for heat and light has been reversed.

(b) **Record the journal entries needed in the general ledger to**

(i) **Remove the incorrect entries**

Account name	Amount £	Debit ✓	Credit ✓

(ii) **Record the correct entries**

Account name	Amount £	Debit ✓	Credit ✓

Chapter 8

Task 8.1

Given below are four cheques received by Southfield Electrical today, 9 January 20X6.

Check each one thoroughly and make a note in the table provided of any errors or problems that you encounter.

	Comments
Cheque from B B Berry Ltd	
Cheque from Q Q Stores	
Cheque from Dagwell Enterprises	
Cheque from Weller Enterprises	

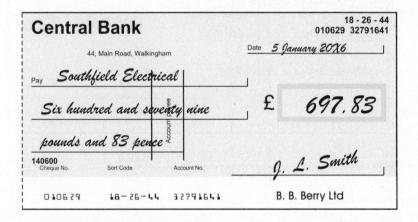

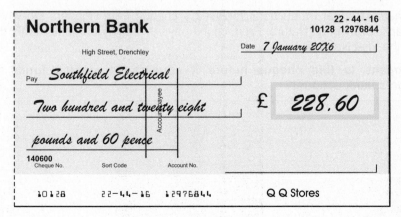

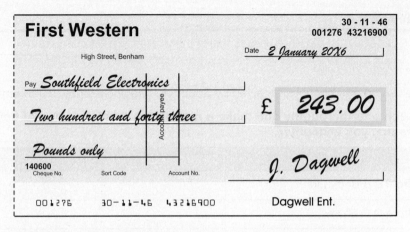

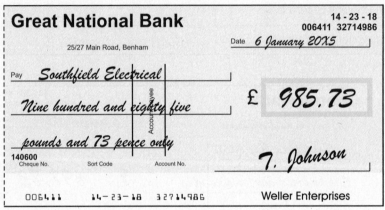

Task 8.2

On 23 January Natural Productions received a cheque from Hoppers Ltd who bank with Central Bank, Drenchley. Natural Productions pays this cheque into its bank, the Benham branch of the First National Bank.

What happens to this cheque before it appears as cleared funds in Natural Production's bank account?

BPP
LEARNING MEDIA

Task 8.3

Given below is the remittance list for Natural Productions for the last week in January, showing cheques received from credit customers and cash from cash sales.

REMITTANCE LIST	
23 Jan	£545.14 from Hoppers Ltd – settlement discount £16.86
23 Jan	£116.70 from Superior Products
24 Jan	£128.46 from cash sales including VAT
24 Jan	£367.20 from Esporta Leisure – settlement discount £11.36
25 Jan	£86.75 from cash sales including VAT
27 Jan	£706.64 from Body Perfect – settlement discount £21.86
27 Jan	£58.90 from cash sales including VAT
27 Jan	£267.90 from Langans Beauty

All of the cheques are to be paid into the bank today, 27 January.

The cash in the till from the cash sales is made up of the following notes and coins:

Notes/coins	Number
£20	5
£10	12
£5	13
£2	1
£1	17
50p	9
20p	4
10p	15
5p	12
2p	16
1p	19

This is all to be paid into the bank other than the cash float which is always made up as follows:

Notes/coins	Number
£10	2
£5	2
£2	0
£1	5
50p	2
10p	10
5p	10
2p	10
1p	10

You are required to fill in the paying-in slip below for payment of the cheques and cash into the bank.

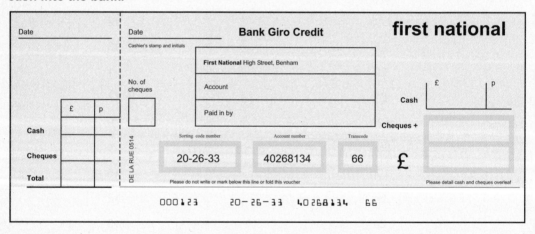

Task 8.4

Your firm, Parker Paints, has received the following BACS remittance advice:

BACS Remittance Advice

To: Parker Paints   From: Handyman Tools Ltd

Your invoice number 1214 dated 15 October for £2,350 has been paid by BACS credit transfer and will arrive in your bank account on 1 December.

(a) **What is the earliest date these funds will be available to Parker Paints?**

[blank box]

(b) **Give ONE advantage to Parker Paints of being paid in this way.**

[blank box]

Task 8.5

Complete the following sentences by inserting the relevant banking terms.

(a) A [blank] would be set up to repay a bank loan in equal monthly instalments.

(b) A [blank] would be set up to make the minimum payment on a credit card by variable amounts each month.

(c) A bank [blank] would be arranged when short-term borrowing is needed.

Task 8.6

Which TWO of the documents below are banking documents that must be retained?

	✓
Statements from suppliers	
Remittance advice notes	
Orders from customers	
Direct debit agreements	
Credit notes from suppliers	
Cheque counterfoils	
Invoices to customers	

Task 8.7

Which TWO of the following items should be checked when a cheque is accepted as payment from customers?

	✓
Funds are available in customer's account	
Issue number	
Words and figures match	
Security number	
Expiry date	
Date is not in the future	

Task 8.8

An organisation that uses deposits made by savers to make loans secured by mortgages on residential property is

	✓
A bank	
A building society	

Answer bank

Answer bank

Basic Accounting II Answer bank

Chapter 1

Task 1.1

The correct answer is: £68.34

....

Task 1.2

Debit side			Credit side								
Date	Details	Amount	Date	Details	Voucher number	Total	VAT	Travel	Post	Stationery	Office supplies
		£				£	£	£	£	£	£
22 Jan	Bal b/f	120.00	23 Jan	Coffee	0721	3.99					3.99
			23 Jan	Stamps	0722	24.00			24.00		
			24 Jan	Taxi fare	0723	10.72	1.78	8.94			
			24 Jan	Paper	0724	7.12	1.18			5.94	
			26 Jan	Train fare	0725	13.60		13.60			
			27 Jan	Disks	0726	11.22	1.87				9.35
						70.65	4.83	22.54	24.00	5.94	13.34

Cross-cast check:

	£
Office supplies	13.34
Stationery	5.94
Post	24.00
Travel	22.54
VAT	4.83
Total	70.65

....

Task 1.3

(a) The correct answer is: £16

Working

	£
Opening balance	22
Cash from bank	53
Less:	
expenditure during month	(16)
balance at end of month	59

Therefore 75 – 59 = £16 required to restore the imprest level

(b) The correct answer is: Debit

Task 1.4

(a)

	Voucher total
	£
0473	12.60
0474	15.00
0475	19.75
0476	9.65
0477	10.00
0478	13.84
0479	4.26
0480	16.40
	101.50

Petty cash box

		£
£10 note	1	10.00
£5 note	4	20.00
£2 coin	3	6.00
£1 coin	7	7.00
50p coin	5	2.50
20p coin	8	1.60
10p coin	9	0.90
5p coin	4	0.20
2p coin	11	0.22
1p coin	8	0.08
		48.50

	£
Voucher total	101.50
Petty cash in the box	48.50
Imprest amount	150.00

(b)

Petty cash control

		£			£
1 Jan	Balance b/f	150.00	31 Jan	Expenditure	101.50
			31 Jan	Balance c/d	48.50
		150.00			150.00
1 Feb	Balance b/d	48.50			

Task 1.5

Date	Details	Amount £	Date	Details	Total £	Stationery £	Postage £	Motor fuel £
1 Nov	Bal b/f	100	7 Nov	Postage stamps	20		20	
			15 Nov	Pens and pencils	18	18		
			22 Nov	Petrol	10			10
			30 Nov	Envelopes	15	15		
					63	33	20	10
			30 Nov	Bal c/d	37			
	Total	100		Total	100			
1 Dec	Bal b/d	37						

Task 1.6

Petty cash book

Debit side		Credit side					
Details	Amount £	Details	Amount £	VAT £	Postage £	Travel £	Cleaning £
Balance b/f	175.00	Post Office	30.00		30.00		
		Window cleaning	30.72	5.12			25.60
		MegaBus	29.50			29.50	
		Balance c/d	84.78				
	175.00		175.00	5.12	30.00	29.50	25.60

Task 1.7

(a)

Petty cash voucher		
Date:	13.9.XX	
Number:	PC331	
Cleaning materials		
Net	£	26.50
VAT	£	5.30
Gross	£	31.80

Petty cash voucher		
Date:	13.9.XX	
Number:	PC332	
Courier costs		
Net	£	51.75
VAT	£	10.35
Gross	£	62.10

(b)

Amount in petty cash box	£	91.70
Balance on petty cash control account	£	96.70
Difference	£	5.00

(c)

Petty cash reimbursement		
Date: 30.09.20XX		
Amount required to restore the cash in the petty cash box	£	240.24

Task 1.8

(a) – (b)

Petty cash book

Debit side		Credit side					
Details	Amount £	Details	Amount £	VAT £	Postage £	Travel £	Stationery £
Balance b/f	150.00	Tom's Taxi	18.00			18.00	
		Post Office	30.00		30.00		
		SMP Stationery	43.20	7.20			36.00
		Balance c/d	58.80				
	150.00		150.00	7.20	30.00	18.00	36.00

Task 1.9

(a)

Petty cash voucher		
Date:	07.XX	
Number:	PC187	
5 packs A4 envelopes		
Net	£	14.00
VAT	£	2.80
Gross	£	16.80

Petty cash voucher		
Date:	7.07.XX	
Number:	PC188	
Fuel for motor van		
Net	£	32.00
VAT	£	6.40
Gross	£	38.40

(b)

Amount in petty cash box	£	116.15
Balance on petty cash control account	£	120.00
Difference	£	3.85

(c)

Petty cash reimbursement		
Date: 31.07.20XX		
Amount required to restore the cash in the petty cash box	£	196.55

Chapter 2

Task 2.1

Who is the drawee?	First National Bank
Who is the payee?	J Peterson
Who is the drawer?	F Ronald

Task 2.2

Date	Details	Cheque No	Discounts received £	Bank £	VAT £	Cash purchases £	Purchases ledger £
10 Jul	W J Jones	002156	10.50	521.36			521.36
10 Jul	Cash purchase	002157		415.80	69.30	346.50	
11 Jul	Trenter Ltd	002158		358.65			358.65
11 Jul	Packing Supp	002159	26.30	754.36			754.36
11 Jul	Cash purchase	002160		85.80	14.30	71.50	
12 Jul	P J Phillips	002161		231.98			231.98
13 Jul	O & P Ltd	002162	17.56	721.30			721.30
14 Jul	Cash purchase	002163		107.52	17.92	89.60	
			54.36	3,196.77	101.52	507.60	2,587.65

Cross-cast check:

	£
Purchases ledger	2,587.65
Cash purchases	507.60
VAT	101.52
Total	3,196.77

Task 2.3

Cash book

Date	Details	Cheque No	Discounts received £	Bank £	VAT £	Purchases ledger £	Rent & rates £
27 Jan	Henson Press	003014		329.00		329.00	
27 Jan	Ely Instruments	003015	12.80	736.96		736.96	
27 Jan	Jester Press	003016	4.47	144.67		144.67	
27 Jan	CD Supplies	003017	1.96	74.54		74.54	
27 Jan	Jester Press	003018	1.38	44.79		44.79	
27 Jan	Buser Ltd	003019	12.25	273.48		273.48	
27 Jan	Rates	SO		255.00			255.00
27 Jan	Rent	DD		500.00			500.00
			32.86	2,358.44		1,603.44	755.00

Cross-cast check:

	£
Rent & rates	755.00
Purchases ledger	1,603.44
Total	2,358.44

···

Task 2.4

Cash book

Date	Details	Discounts allowed £	Cash £	Bank £	VAT £	Cash sales £	Sales ledger £
10 Jul	Superior Products	32.56		891.36			891.36
11 Jul	Hoppers Ltd			295.68			295.68
11 Jul	Cash sales		138.24		23.04	115.20	
13 Jul	Body Perfect	21.45		542.97			542.97
13 Jul	Cash sales		209.76		34.96	174.80	
14 Jul	Esporta Leisure	42.58		958.45			958.45
14 Jul	Cash sales		84.48		14.08	70.40	
14 Jul	Langans Beauty			752.45			752.45
		96.59	432.48	3,440.91	72.08	360.40	3,440.91

BPP
LEARNING MEDIA

Cross-cast check:

	£
Sales ledger	3,440.91
Cash sales	360.40
VAT	72.08
Total	3,873.39
Cash	432.48
Bank	3,440.91
Total	3,873.39

Task 2.5

(a) Cash book – credit side

Details	Discounts £	Cash £	Bank £	VAT £	Purchases ledger £	Cash purchases £	Stationery £
Balance b/f			236				
Dubai Dreams		324		54		270	
Walter Enterprises		228		38		190	
Sinead Reilly		56				56	
Sumatra Trading	35		7,265		7,265		
SHSK Co			378	63			315
Total	35	608	7,879	155	7,265	516	315

(b)

Details	Discounts £	Cash £	Bank £	Sales ledger £
Balance b/f		1,228		
Park Farm Stores			2,576	2,576
Tristram Pale Ltd	25		4,233	4,233
Total	25	1,228	6,809	6,809

(c) The correct answer is: £620

   Working

   (1,228 – 608)

(d) The correct answer is: £1,070

   Working

   (7,879 – 6,809)

(e) The correct answer is: Credit

Task 2.6

(a) **Cash book – credit side**

Details	Discount £	Cash £	Bank £	VAT £	Purchases ledger £	Cash purchases £	Motor expenses £
Balance b/f			16,942				
B Smithson Ltd		240		40		200	
H Hamnet		192		32		160	
Renee Reid		320				320	
Tenon Ltd	80		3,600		3,600		
Vernon Motor Repairs			48	8			40
Total	80	752	20,590	80	3,600	680	40

(b) **Cash book – debit side**

Details	Discount £	Cash £	Bank £	Sales ledger £
Balance b/f		1,325		
G Brownlow			749	749
S Barnett	30		300	300
Total	30	1,325	1,049	1,049

(c) The correct answer is: £573

Working

(1,325 – 752 = 573)

(d) The correct answer is: £19,541

Working

(20,590 – 1,049 = 19,541)

(e) The correct answer is: Credit

Chapter 3

Task 3.1

Transaction	Debit ✓	Credit ✓
£470.47 paid into the bank		✓
Standing order of £26.79	✓	
Cheque payment of £157.48	✓	
Interest earned on the bank balance		✓
BACS payment for wages	✓	

Task 3.2

Cash book – debit side

Date	Details	Discounts allowed £	Bank £	VAT £	Sales ledger £	Music sales £	Instrument sales £	CD sales £	Interest £
	Bal b/f		379.22						
27 Jan	Tunfield DC		594.69		594.69				
27 Jan	Tunshire CO	14.48	468.29		468.29				
27 Jan	Non-credit sales		478.90			478.90			
27 Jan	Tunfield BB	33.03	1,059.72		1,059.72				
27 Jan	Non-credit sales		752.16	125.36			626.80		
27 Jan	Non-credit sales		256.80	42.80				214.00	
		47.51	3,989.78	168.16	2,122.70	478.90	626.80	214.00	

Task 3.3

Unmatched item	Action to be taken
Bank Giro Credit Tunfield AOS	This must be checked to any supporting documentation such as any remittance advice from Tunfield AOS or the original invoice – when it has been checked the amount should be entered into the cash book
Standing order to British Elec	The standing order schedule should be checked to ensure that this is correct and it should then be entered into the cash book
Bank interest received	This should be entered into the cash book
Sales of CDs	The £256.80 cash sales of CDs settled by cheque do not appear on the bank statement. This is a reconciling item
Cheque number 003016	Unpresented cheque – will appear in the bank reconciliation statement
Cheque number 003018	Unpresented cheque – will appear in the bank reconciliation statement
Cheque number 003019	Unpresented cheque – will appear in the bank reconciliation statement

Task 3.4

Cash book – debit side

Date	Details	Discounts allowed £	Bank £	VAT £	Sales ledger £	Music sales £	Instrument sales £	CD sales £	Interest £
	Balance b/f		379.22						
27 Jan	Tunfield DC		594.69✓		594.69				
27 Jan	Tunshire CO	14.48	468.29✓		468.29				
27 Jan	Non-credit sales		478.90✓				478.90		
27 Jan	Tunfield BB	33.03	1,059.72✓		1,059.72				
27 Jan	Non-credit sales		752.16✓	125.36			626.80		
27 Jan	Non-credit sales		256.80	42.80				214.00	
27 Jan	Bank interest		3.68						3.68
27 Jan	Tunfield AOS	——	108.51	——	108.51	——	——	——	——
		47.51	4,101.97	168.16	2,231.21	478.90	626.80	214.00	3.68

Cash book – credit side

Date	Cheque no.	Details	Discounts received £	Bank £	VAT £	Purchases ledger £	Rent & rates £	Sundry £
27 Jan	003014	Henson Press		329.00✓		329.00		
27 Jan	003015	Ely Instr	12.80	736.96✓		736.96		
27 Jan	003016	Jester Press	4.47	144.67		144.67		
27 Jan	003017	CD Supplies	1.96	74.54✓		74.54		
27 Jan	003018	Jester Press	1.38	44.79		44.79		
27 Jan	003019	Buser Ltd	12.25	273.48		273.48		
27 Jan	SO	Rates		255.00✓			255.00	
27 Jan	DD	Rent		500.00✓			500.00	
27 Jan	SO	British Elec		212.00✓				212.00
27 Jan		Balance c/d		1,531.53				
			32.86	4,101.97		1,603.44	755.00	212.00

Task 3.5

Bank reconciliation statement as at 27 January

	£	£
Balance per bank statement		1,737.67
Outstanding lodgement		256.80
Total to add		1,994.47
Unpresented cheques		
003016	144.67	
003018	44.79	
003019	273.48	
Total to subtract		(462.94)
Amended cash book balance		1,531.53

Task 3.6

Cash book

Date	Details	Bank £	Date	Cheque no.	Details	Bank £
01 Nov	Balance b/f	5,466	03 Nov	110870	Roberts & Co	6,250
24 Nov	Bevan & Co	1,822	03 Nov	110871	J Jones	1,164
24 Nov	Plant Pots Ltd	7,998	06 Nov	110872	Lake Walks Ltd	2,250
21 Nov	BBT Ltd	10,000	10 Nov	110873	PH Supplies	275
24 Nov	Petals Ltd	2,555	17 Nov	110874	Peters & Co	76
			21 Nov	DD	Insurance Ensured	500
			24 Nov	DD	Rainbow Ltd	88
			28 Nov		Balance c/d	17,238
		27,841				27,841
29 Nov	Balance b/d	17,238				

Note: cheque number 110865 on the bank statement: the first cheque in the cash book in November is number 110870. As the difference between the opening balances on the bank statement and in the cash book is for the amount of this cheque (£3,670) it is reasonable to assume that cheque 110865 was entered in the cash book in a previous month and would have been a reconciling item in the bank reconciliation in the previous month. This cheque should be ticked to the October bank reconciliation.

Bank reconciliation statement as at 28 November

	£
Balance per bank statement:	7,769
Add:	
Name: Bevan & Co	1,822
Name: Plant Pots Ltd	7,998
Total to add	9,820
Less:	
Name: PH Supplies	275
Name: Peters & Co	76
Total to subtract	351
Balance as per cash book	17,238

Task 3.7

(a) The correct answers are: Outstanding lodgements and Unpresented cheques. The other two items are amended in the cash book.

(b) The correct answer is: £657 overdrawn

   Working

   £ (565) o/d + £92 dishonoured cheque = £ (657) o/d

(c) The correct answer is: £6,450 overdrawn

   Workings

	£	£
Balance b/f		5,675
Reversal – Standing order entered twice	125	
Reversal – Dishonoured cheque entered in error as a debit		450
Correction – Dishonoured cheque		450
Balance c/d (overdraft)	6,450	
	6,575	6,575

(d) The correct answer is: £2,300

   Workings

	£
Cash book balance	2,490
Adjustment re charges	(50)
Adjustment re dishonoured cheque from customer	(140)
	2,300

(e) The correct answer is: Cheques issued for £250 recorded in the cash book, but not yet gone through the bank account

   All the other options would have the bank account £250 less than the cash book.

(f)   The correct answer is: £3,366

Workings

	£
Balance per cash book	3,526
Plus: bank interest received	150
Less: dishonoured cheque	(310)
Amended cash book balance	3,366

· ·

Task 3.8

Cash book

Date 20XX	Details	Bank £	Date 20XX	Cheque number	Details	Bank £
01 Jul	Balance b/f	1,855	01 Jul	126459	Gumpley Co	3,283
20 Jul	Brimfull Ltd	5,483	01 Jul	126460	Warnes Ltd	1,209
21 Jul	Adera Ltd	2,198	01 Jul	126461	Veldt Partners	4,221
22 Jul	Mist Northern	1,004	01 Jul	126462	Pathways	1,117
9 Jul	Snip Snap Co	8,845	02 Jul	126463	Lindstrom Co	846
			02 Jul	126464	Kestrels Training	658
			13 Jul	126465	HGW Ltd	3,200
			13 Jul		Flit DC	500
			18 Jul		Consol Landlords	475
			20 Jul		Bank charges	32
			22 Jul		Interest	103
			23 Jul		Balance c/d	3,741
		19,385				19,385
24 Jul	Balance b/d	3,741				

Bank reconciliation statement as at 23 July 20XX

Balance per bank statement		£	4,585
Add:			
Name:	Adera Ltd	£	2,198
Name:	Mist Northern	£	1,004
Total to add		£	3,202
Less:			
Name:	Lindstrom Co	£	846
Name:	HGW Ltd	£	3,200
Total to subtract		£	4,046
Balance as per cash book		£	3,741

Chapter 4

Task 4.1

Sales ledger control

	£		£
Balance b/f	11,689	Sales returns	1,582
Sales	12,758	Bank	11,563
Bank (dishonoured cheque)	722	Discounts allowed	738
		Irrecoverable debt written off	389
		Balance c/d	10,897
	25,169		25,169

Task 4.2

Purchases ledger control

	£		£
Purchases returns	728	Balance b/f	8,347
Bank	8,837	Purchases	9,203
Discounts received	382		
Balance c/d	7,603		
	17,550		17,550

Task 4.3

Purchases ledger control

Date	Details	Amount £	Date	Details	Amount £
30 June	Bank	33,106	1 June	Balance b/f	85,299
30 June	Discounts received	1,000	30 June	Purchases	39,300
30 June	Purchases returns	275			
30 June	Balance c/d	90,218			
		124,599			124,599
			1 July	Balance b/d	90,218

Task 4.4

(a) The correct answer is: £32,125

Working

£31,475 + £125,000 − £122,500 − £550 − £1,300 = £32,125 debit

(b) The correct answer is: £38,100

Working

	£
Opening balance	34,500
Credit purchases	78,400
Discounts received	(1,200)
Payments	(68,900)
Purchases returns	(4,700)
	38,100

Task 4.5

	Bank	SLCA £	PLCA £	VAT £	Purchases £	Sales returns £	Discounts received £	Discounts allowed £
	DR/CR	DR/CR	DR/CR	DR/CR	DR/CR	DR/CR	DR/CR	DR/CR
Gross credit purchases £3,390			3,390 CR	565 DR	2,825 DR			
Gross credit sales returns £1,860		1,860 CR		310 DR		1,550 DR		
Payments to credit suppliers £4,590	4,590 CR		4,590 DR					
Receipts from credit customers £5,480	5,480 DR	5,480 CR						
Discounts allowed £400		400 CR						400 DR
Discounts received £200			200 DR				200 CR	

Task 4.6

Account name	Amount £	Debit ✓	Credit ✓
Irrecoverable debts	1,560	✓	
VAT	312	✓	
Sales ledger control	1,872		✓

Chapter 5

Task 5.1

	Control account	List of balances	Both
	✓	✓	✓
Invoice entered into the sales day book as £980 instead of £890			✓
Purchases day book overcast by £1,000	✓		
Discounts allowed of £20 not entered into the cash book (debit side)			✓
An invoice taken as £340 instead of £440 when being posted to the customer's account		✓	
Incorrect balancing of a memorandum ledger account		✓	
A purchases return not entered into the purchases returns day book			✓

Task 5.2

Sales ledger control

	£		£
Balance b/f	5,000	Bank (2,400 + 3,600 +1,100 + 4,800)	
			11,900
Sales (2,000 + 2,700 + 1,100 + 3,800)	9,600		
		Balance c/d	2,700
	14,600		14,600
Balance b/d	2,700		

Sales ledger

H Simms

	£		£
Balance b/f	900	Bank	2,400
Sales	2,000	Balance c/d	500
	2,900		2,900
Balance b/d	500		

P Good

	£		£
Balance b/f	1,600	Bank	3,600
Sales	2,700	Balance c/d	700
	4,300		4,300
Balance b/d	700		

K Mitchell

	£		£
Sales	1,100	Bank	1,100

C Brown

	£		£
Balance b/f	2,500	Bank	4,800
Sales	3,800	Balance c/d	1,500
	6,300		6,300
Balance b/d	1,500		

Reconciliation of sales ledger balances with control account balance

	£
H Simms	500
P Good	700
K Mitchell	
C Brown	1,500
Sales ledger control account	2,700

Task 5.3

Purchases ledger control

	£		£
Bank		Balance b/f	2,700
(1,700 + 3,200 + 3,000)	7,900	Purchases	
Balance c/d	2,100	(1,600 + 2,500 + 3,200)	7,300
	10,000		10,000
		Balance b/d	2,100

Purchases ledger

J Peters

	£		£
Bank	1,700	Balance b/f	300
Balance c/d	200	Purchases	1,600
	1,900		1,900
		Balance b/d	200

T Sands

	£		£
Bank	3,200	Balance b/f	1,700
Balance c/d	1,000	Purchases	2,500
	4,200		4,200
		Balance b/d	1,000

L Farmer

	£		£
Bank	3,000	Balance b/f	700
Balance c/d	900	Purchases	3,200
	3,900		3,900
		Balance b/d	900

Reconciliation of purchases ledger balances with control account balance

	£
J Peters	200
T Sands	1,000
L Farmer	900
Purchases ledger control account	2,100

Task 5.4

Sales ledger control

	£		£
Balance b/f	13,452	(i) Sales returns	100
		(iii) Irrecoverable debts expense	200
		Balance c/d	13,152
	13,452		13,452
Balance b/d	13,152		

	£
Sales ledger list of balances	12,614
Error: (ii) Over-statement of receipt (530 – 350)	180
Error: (iv) Balance omitted	358
Amended list of balances	13,152
Amended control account balance	13,152

Task 5.5

Purchases ledger control

	£		£
(iv) Discounts received: reversal of credit	256	Balance b/f	26,677
(iv) Discounts received: correct entry	256	(i) Purchases	1,000
Balance c/d	27,165		
	27,677		27,677
		Balance b/d	27,165

	£
Purchases ledger list of balances	27,469
Error: (ii) Discounts omitted	(64)
Error: (iii) Debit balance – remove credit balance	(120)
Error: (iii) Debit balance – enter as debit balance	(120)
Amended list of balances	27,165
Amended control account balance	27,165

Task 5.6

(a)

Sales ledger control

Date	Details	Amount £	Date	Details	Amoun £
01 Nov	Balance b/f	48,125	30 Nov	Bank	28,327
30 Nov	Sales	37,008	30 Nov	Discounts allowed	240
			30 Nov	Sales returns	2,316
			30 Nov	Balance c/d	54,250
		85,133			85,133
01 Dec	Balance b/d	54,250			

(b)

	£
Sales ledger control account balance as at 1 December	54,250
Total of sales ledger accounts as at 1 December	(54,163)
Difference	87

(c) The correct answers are: A sales credit note has been entered in the sales ledger twice and A receipt from a customer has been entered in the sales ledger twice

....

Task 5.7

The correct answer is: £313

Working

VAT control

	£		£
Purchases (£4,500 × 20%)	900	Balance b/f	2,165
Van (£10,460 × 20%)	2,092	Sales (£(6,000 – 300) × 20%)	1,140
Balance c/d	313		
	3,305		3,305

....

Task 5.8

The correct answer is: £10,773.50

Workings

	£
VAT on sales (126,900 × 20/120)	21,150.00
Less: VAT on purchases (57,810 × 20/120)	(9,635.00)
VAT on credit notes (2,820 × 20/120)	(470.00)
VAT on expenses	(271.50)
	10,773.50

....

Task 5.9

(a) One of either of the following reasons:
  - Sales were less than purchases during the period.
  - There had been an overpayment of VAT in the previous period.

(b) The correct answer is: £21,540

  Working

  £129,240 × 20/120 = £21,540

....

Task 5.10

(a) The correct answer is: The supplier has allowed you £150 settlement discount which you had not entered in your ledger

  All other options would lead to a higher balance in the supplier's records.

(b) The correct answer is: Both the control account and the list of balances

(c) The correct answer is: £75,355

Working

	£
Balance per listing	81,649
Less: invoice posted twice	(4,688)
Less: payments omitted	(1,606)
	75,355
Balance per control account	76,961
Less: payments omitted	(1,606)
	75,355

....

Task 5.11

(a)   The correct answers are: The balance on the sales ledger control account and The total of all the sales ledger balances

(b)   The correct answer is: Over how many months the outstanding balance owed by each individual credit customer has built up

....

Chapter 6

Task 6.1

(a)   The correct answer is: £297.06

Working

	£
Gross wage	440.00
PAYE income tax	(77.76)
Employees' NIC	(43.18)
Pension contribution (440.00 × 5%)	(22.00)
Net pay	297.06

(b)   The correct answers are:

£297.06 should be paid to Peter

£22.00 should be paid to the pension administrator

£170.29 (£77.76 + £43.18 + £49.35) should be paid to HM Revenue and Customs

(c)

Wages expense

	£		£
Wages control	440.00		
Wages control	49.35		

Wages control

	£		£
Bank	297.06	Wages expense	440.00
PAYE/NIC payable	77.76	Wages expense	49.35
PAYE/NIC payable	43.18		
Pension payable	22.00		
PAYE/NIC payable	49.35		

PAYE/NIC payable

	£		£
		Wages control	77.76
		Wages control	43.18
		Wages control	49.35

Pension payable

	£		£
		Wages control	22.00

Bank

	£		£
		Wages control	297.06

Task 6.2

Journal

Account name	Debit £	Credit £
Capital		10,000
Furniture and fittings	15,315	
Sales		127,318
Motor vehicles	20,109	
Cash at bank	15,000	
Purchases	86,120	
Purchases returns		750
Purchases ledger control		37,238
Sales ledger control	53,259	
Loan from bank		7,000
Motor expenses	1,213	
VAT		8,710
Totals	191,016	191,016

Task 6.3

Journal

Account name	Amount £	Debit ✓	Credit ✓
Irrecoverable debts expense	240	✓	
VAT (£240 × 20% = £48)	48	✓	
Sales ledger control	288		✓

Task 6.4

Journal

Account names	Amount £	Debit ✓	Credit ✓
(a)			
Discounts allowed	50	✓	
Discounts received	50		✓
(b)			
Bank deposit account	200	✓	
Bank current account	200		✓
(c)			
Irrecoverable debts expense	2,800	✓	
VAT control	560	✓	
Sales ledger control	3,360		✓

Task 6.5

Account name	Amount £	Debit ✓	Credit ✓
Irrecoverable debts expense	2,370	✓	
VAT	474	✓	
Sales ledger control	2,844		✓

Task 6.6

Account name	Amount £	Debit ✓	Credit ✓
Petty cash control	200	✓	
Cash at bank	1,000	✓	
Capital	500		✓
Van	6,000	✓	
Trade receivables	7,700	✓	
Loan from bank	9,000		✓
Sales	15,250		✓
Purchases	6,230	✓	
Trade payables	3,400		✓
Expenses	7,020	✓	
Journal to record the opening entries of new business			

Task 6.7

Account name	Amount £	Debit ✓	Credit ✓
Cash	150	✓	
Cash at bank	12,350	✓	
Capital	23,456		✓
Fixtures and fittings	2,100	✓	
Insurance	825	✓	
Loan from bank	10,000		✓
Miscellaneous expenses	218	✓	
Motor vehicle	15,650	✓	
Office expenses	613	✓	
Rent and rates	1,550	✓	
Journal to record the opening entries of new business			

Chapter 7

Task 7.1

Account name	Amount £	Debit ✓	Credit ✓
Suspense	11,081	✓	

Task 7.2

The correct answer is: Discounts allowed of £124 were only posted to the discounts allowed account.

Task 7.3

Sales ledger control

	£		£
Balance b/f	1,683	Bank	14,228
Sales	15,899	Discounts allowed	900
		Irrecoverable debts expense	245
		Sales returns	1,467
		Balance c/d	742
	17,582		17,582

VAT

	£		£
Purchases	1,985	Balance b/f	2,576
		Sales	2,368
Balance c/d	3,074	Purchases returns	115
	5,059		5,059

Task 7.4

(a) Journal entries

			£	£
(i)	Debit	Sales ledger control	1,000	
	Credit	Suspense		1,000
(ii)	Debit	Electricity	1,642	
	Credit	Suspense		1,642
(iii)	Debit	Discounts allowed	865	
	Credit	Suspense		865
	Debit	Discounts allowed	865	
	Credit	Suspense		865
(iv)	Debit	Sales ledger control	360	
	Credit	Bank		360
(v)	Debit	Purchases ledger control	120	
	Credit	Discounts received		120

(b)

Suspense

	£		£
Balance b/f	4,372	(i) Sales ledger control	1,000
		(ii) Electricity	1,642
		(iii) Discounts allowed × 2	1,730
	4,372		4,372

Task 7.5

The journal

Account names	Debit £	Credit £
(a) Sales returns	500	
Sales		500
(b) Office expenses	125	
Bank		125
Office expenses	125	
Bank		125
(c) Bank	29	
Suspense	270	
Purchases		299
Purchases	299	
Bank		299
(d) Sales ledger control	388	
Suspense		388
Discounts allowed	388	
Sales ledger control		388

Task 7.6

Suspense account

Date	Details	Amount £	Date	Details	Amount £
01 July	Sales	945	30 June	Balance b/f	720
			01 July	Bank (rent & rates)	225
		945			945

Task 7.7

(a) The correct answer is: Credit £90

£890 should have been debited to the expense account. Instead, £980 has been debited. To bring this amount down to £890, the expense account should be credited with £90.

(b) The correct answer is: Error of omission

(c) The correct answer is: One side of a transaction has been recorded in the wrong account, and that account is of the same class as the correct account

(d) The correct answer is: The purchase of a non-current asset debited to the purchases account and credited to the supplier's account

(e) The correct answer is: Original entry

(f) The correct answer is: Debit £1,350

Workings

Suspense account

	£		£
Opening balance	1,350	Discounts allowed	7,500
Discounts received	6,150		
	7,500		7,500

(g) The correct answer is: The debit side to be £96 more than the credit side

Working

Debits will exceed credits by 2 × £48 = £96

(h)

	Yes	No
Omitting both entries for a transaction		✓
Posting the debit entry for an invoice to an incorrect expense account		✓
Omitting the debit entry for a transaction	✓	
Posting the debit entry for a transaction as a credit entry	✓	

Task 7.8

Error in the general ledger	Error disclosed by the trial balance ✓	Error NOT disclosed by the trial balance ✓
Recording a bank receipt of a cash sale on the debit side of the cash sales account	✓	
Entering an insurance expense in the administration expenses account		✓
Entering the discounts received account balance on the debit side of the trial balance	✓	
Miscasting the total column of one page of the sales returns day book	✓	
Failing to write up a dishonoured cheque in the cash book		✓
Recording discount allowed of £15 as £150 in the cash book		✓

Task 7.9

Discounts allowed

Details	Amount £	Details	Amount £
Suspense	209		

Machinery

Details	Amount £	Details	Amount £
		Motor vehicles	4,300

Motor vehicles

Details	Amount £	Details	Amount £
Machinery	4,300		

Sales ledger control

Details	Amount £	Details	Amount £
		Suspense	750

Suspense

Details	Amount £	Details	Amount £
Sales ledger control	750	Balance b/f	541
		Discounts allowed	209

Task 7.10

	Balances extracted on 30 June £	Balances at 1 July	
		Debit £	Credit £
Machinery	82,885	82,885	
Computer equipment	41,640	41,640	
Insurance	17,520	17,520	
Bank overdraft	13,252		13,252
Petty cash	240	240	
Sales ledger control	241,500	247,250	
Purchases ledger control	134,686		134,686
VAT owing to HM Revenue and Customs	19,920		19,920
Capital	44,826		44,826
Sales	525,092		525,092
Purchases	269,400	269,400	
Purchases returns	16,272		16,272
Wages	61,680	61,680	
Maintenance expenses	3,283	3,283	
Stationery	8,049	8,049	
Rent and rates	3,466	3,466	
Heat and light	5,172	5,712	
Telephone	7,596	7,596	
Marketing expenses	5,327	5,327	
Suspense (debit balance)	6,290		
Totals		754,048	754,048

Task 7.11

(a)

(i) Remove the correct entry

Account name	Amount £	Debit ✓	Credit ✓
VAT	1,100		✓

(ii) Record the correct entry

Account name	Amount £	Debit ✓	Credit ✓
VAT	1,000	✓	

(iii) Remove the suspense account balance

Account name	Amount £	Debit ✓	Credit ✓
Suspense	100	✓	

(b)

(i) Remove the incorrect entries

Account name	Amount £	Debit ✓	Credit ✓
Heat and light	350	✓	
Bank	350		✓

(ii) Record the correct entries

Account name	Amount £	Debit ✓	Credit ✓
Heat and light	350	✓	
Bank	350		✓

Chapter 8

Task 8.1

	Comments
Cheque from B B Berry Ltd	Words and figures differ
Cheque from Q Q Stores	Unsigned
Cheque from Dagwell Enterprises	Payee name is incorrect – Electronics instead of Electrical
Cheque from Weller Enterprises	Dated 6 January 20X5 instead of 20X6 – this cheque is therefore out of date

Task 8.2

Day 1

The Benham branch of First National sends the cheque to the First National clearing department in London.

Day 2

The First National clearing department sorts all of the cheques received by bank.

The cheque from Hoppers Ltd is sent to the Central Clearing House together with the other cheques received by First National which have been drawn on Central Bank.

The cheque is then sent to the clearing department of Central Bank which sends the cheque to the Drenchley branch of Central Bank.

Day 3

Provided the cheque is valid and correct it is then paid out of Hoppers Ltd's account and credited to Natural Productions' account.

Task 8.3

Calculation of cash to be paid into the bank:

Cash in till Notes/coins	Number	Float required	Paid into bank	Total £
£20	5	–	5	100.00
£10	12	2	10	100.00
£5	13	2	11	55.00
£2	1	–	1	2.00
£1	17	5	12	12.00
50p	9	2	7	3.50
20p	4	–	4	0.80
10p	15	10	5	0.50
5p	12	10	2	0.10
2p	16	10	6	0.12
1p	19	10	9	0.09
				274.11

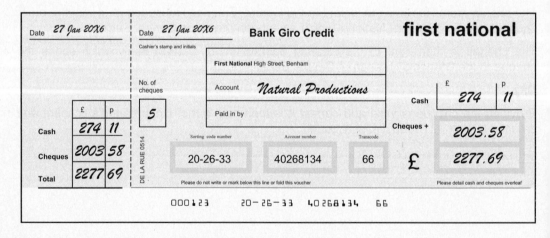

BPP
LEARNING MEDIA

Task 8.4

(a) The correct answer is: 1 December

With a BACS transfer there is no clearing period therefore the money is available immediately.

(b) The correct answer is ONE of:

There is no cheque to pay in at the bank so no need to visit the bank

Time-saving as no paying-in slip required

Greater security as no physical handling of the payment

No time delay due to the clearing system

Task 8.5

(a) A ┃ standing order ┃ would be set up to repay a bank loan in equal monthly instalments.

(b) A ┃ direct debt ┃ would be set up to make the minimum payment on a credit card by variable amounts each month.

(c) A bank ┃ overdraft ┃ would be arranged when short-term borrowing is needed.

Task 8.6

The correct answers are: Direct debit agreements and Cheque counterfoils

Task 8.7

The correct answers are: Words and figures match, and Date is not in the future

Task 8.8

The correct answer is: A building society

Answer bank

AAT PRACTICE ASSESSMENT 1
BASIC ACCOUNTING II

Time allowed: 2 hours

AAT PRACTICE
ASSESSMENT 1

Basic Accounting II AAT practice assessment 1

Section 1

Task 1.1

Kitchen Kuts' trial balance was extracted and did not balance. The debit column of the trial balance totalled £400,278 and the credit column totalled £420,125.

(a) **What entry would be made in the suspense account to balance the trial balance?**

Account name	Amount £	Debit ✓	Credit ✓
Suspense			

It is important to understand the types of error that are disclosed by the trial balance and those that are not.

(b) **Show which of the errors below are, or are not, disclosed by the trial balance.**

Error in the general ledger	Error disclosed by the trial balance ✓	Error NOT disclosed by the trial balance ✓
Recording a bank payment for heat and light on the debit side of both the bank and heat and light account		
Recording a payment for motor repairs in the motor vehicles account		
Recording a sales credit note on the debit side of the sales ledger control account and the credit side of the sales returns account		
Incorrectly calculating the balance on the rent account		
Recording a payment by cheque to a trade payable in the bank account and purchases ledger only		
Recording a bank payment of £470 for motor repairs as £4,700 in both accounts		

Task 1.2

A credit customer, Gaulton Ltd, has ceased trading, owing Gold Ltd £1,680 plus VAT.

(a) **Record the journal entries needed in the general ledger to write off the net amount and the VAT.**

Account name		Amount £	Debit ✓	Credit ✓
	▼			
	▼			
	▼			

Picklist:

Gaulton Ltd
Gold Ltd
Irrecoverable debts
Purchases
Purchases ledger control
Sales
Sales ledger control
VAT

(b) Gold Ltd has started a new business, Metal Craft Ltd, and a new set of accounts is to be opened. A partially completed journal to record the opening entries is shown below.

Record the journal entries needed in the accounts in the general ledger of Metal Craft Ltd to deal with the opening entries.

Account name	Amount £	Debit ✓	Credit ✓
Commission received	175		
Office equipment	1,555		
Bank	368		
Sales	3,500		
Capital	7,967		
Office expenses	876		
Loan from bank	15,000		
Purchases	4,754		
Motor vehicle	18,632		
Motor vehicle expenses	457		
Journal to record the opening entries of new business			

....

Task 1.3

Kitchen Kuts pays its employees by cheque every month and maintains a wages control account. A summary of last month's payroll transactions is shown below:

Item	£
Gross wages	6,236
Employer's NI	730
Employees' NI	620
Income tax	1,808
Trade Union fees	300

Record the journal entries needed in the general ledger to:

(a) **Record the wages expense**

Account name	Amount £	Debit ✓	Credit ✓
▼			
▼			

(b) **Record the HM Revenue and Customs liability**

Account name	Amount £	Debit ✓	Credit ✓
▼			
▼			

(c) **Record the net wages paid to the employees**

Account name	Amount £	Debit ✓	Credit ✓
▼			
▼			

(d) **Record the Trade Union liability**

Account name	Amount £	Debit ✓	Credit ✓
▼			
▼			

Picklist for line items:

Bank
Employees' NI
Employer's NI
HM Revenue and Customs
Income tax
Net wages
Trade Union
Wages control
Wages expense

Task 1.4

Gold Ltd's initial trial balance includes a suspense account with a balance of £2,160.

The error has been traced to the cash book shown below.

Cash book

Date 20XX	Details	Bank £	Date 20XX	Details	VAT £	Bank £
30 Jun	Balance b/f	1,864	30 Jun	Cameron Arts (trade payable)		985
30 Jun	Tsang Traders (trade receivable)	2,200	30 Jun	Miscellaneous expenses	240	1,440
			30 Jun	Motor expenses		246
			30 Jun	Balance c/d		1,393
	Totals	4,064			2,400	4,064

(a) **Identify the error and record the journal entries needed in the general ledger to**

   (i) **Remove the incorrect entry**

Account name	Amount £	Debit ✓	Credit ✓
▼			

   (ii) **Record the correct entry**

Account name	Amount £	Debit ✓	Credit ✓
▼			

   (iii) **Remove the suspense account balance**

Account name	Amount £	Debit ✓	Credit ✓
▼			

Picklist for line items:

Bank
Cameron Arts
Cash
Miscellaneous expenses
Motor expenses
Purchases
Purchases ledger control
Sales
Sales ledger control
Suspense
Tsang Traders
VAT

An entry to record a bank payment of £352 for premises repairs (VAT not applicable) has been reversed.

(b) **Record the journal entries needed in the general ledger to**

(i) **Remove the incorrect entry**

Account name	Amount £	Debit ✓	Credit ✓
▼			
▼			

(ii) **Record the correct entry**

Account name	Amount £	Debit ✓	Credit ✓
▼			
▼			

Picklist for line items:

Bank
Cash
Premises repairs
Purchases
Purchases ledger control
Sales
Sales ledger control
Suspense
VAT

Task 1.5

Kitchen Kuts' trial balance included a suspense account. All the bookkeeping errors have now been traced and the journal entries shown below have been recorded.

Journal entries

Account name	Debit £	Credit £
Office stationery	167	
Suspense		167
Suspense	1,800	
Rent and rates		1,800
Bank interest received	98	
Bank interest charged		98

Use the relevant drag items to post the journal entries to the general ledger accounts. Where there is more than one entry in an account you should make the entries in the same order as given in the task.

Office stationery

Details	Amount £	Details	Amount £

Rent and rates

Details	Amount £	Details	Amount £

Suspense

Details	Amount £	Details	Amount £
		Balance b/f	1,633

Bank interest received

Details	Amount £	Details	Amount £

Bank interest charged

Details	Amount £	Details	Amount £

Drag items for Details:

Bank interest charged
Bank interest received
Office stationery
Rent and rates
Suspense
Suspense

Drag items for £:

98
98
167
167
1,800
1,800

Task 1.6

On 30 June Kitchen Kuts extracted an initial trial balance which did not balance, and a suspense account was opened with a £10,952 debit balance. On 1 July journal entries were prepared to correct the errors that had been found, and clear the suspense account. The list of balances in the initial trial balance, and the journal entries to correct the errors, are shown below.

Re-draft the trial balance by placing the figures in the debit or credit column. You should take into account the journal entries which will clear the suspense account. Do not enter figures with decimal places in this task.

Journal entries

Account name	Debit £	Credit £
Bank	5,521	
Suspense		5,521
Bank	5,521	
Suspense		5,521

Account name	Debit £	Credit £
Purchases returns	6,780	
Suspense		6,780
Purchases returns		6,870
Suspense	6,870	

	Balances extracted on 30 June £	Balances at 1 July Debit £	Credit £
Motor vehicles	34,536		
Fixtures and fittings	17,350		
Inventory	7,300		
Bank overdraft	5,521		
Petty cash	100		
Sales ledger control	100,625		
Purchases ledger control	56,119		
VAT owing to HM Revenue and Customs	8,300		
Capital	22,844		
Sales	222,955		
Purchases	112,250		
Purchases returns	6,780		
Wages	25,700		
Motor expenses	1,368		
Office expenses	3,354		
Rent and rates	1,444		
Heat and light	2,155		
Insurance	3,165		
Miscellaneous expenses	2,220		
Totals			

Section 2

Task 2.1

There are five payments to be entered in Gold Ltd's cash book.

Cash purchases listing

Suppliers paid in cash	Net £	VAT £	Gross £
JBL Ltd	200	40	240
Bocelli Brothers	280	56	336

Trade payables payment listing

Credit suppliers paid by cheque	Amount paid £	Discount taken £
B and B Boards	376	
Rosen Ltd	1,890	38

Cheque book counterfoil (stub)

Bache Builders

(We have no credit account with this supplier)

£1,128 including VAT

001311

(a) **Enter the details from the cash purchases listing, the trade payables payment listing and the cheque book counterfoil (stub) into the credit side of the cash book shown below and total each column.**

Cash book – credit side

Details	Discount £	Cash £	Bank £	VAT £	Trade payables £	Cash purchases £	General repairs £
Balance b/f			1,150				
▼							
▼							
▼							
▼							
▼							
Total							

There are two cheques from credit customers to be entered in Gold Ltd's cash book:

Darren Davies   £253

Clarkson Ltd   £812 (this customer has taken a £36 settlement discount)

(b) **Enter the above details into the debit side of the cash book and total each column.**

Cash book – debit side

Details	Discount £	Cash £	Bank £	Trade receivables £
Balance b/f		778		
▼				
▼				
Total				

Picklist:

B and B Boards
Bache Builders
Bocelli Brothers
Clarkson Ltd
Darren Davies
JBL Ltd
Rosen Ltd

(c) **Using your answers to (a) and (b) above, calculate the cash balance.**

£

(d) **Using your answers to (a) and (b) above, calculate the bank balance. If your calculations show that the bank account is overdrawn your answer should start with a minus sign for example, –123.**

£

(e) **Will the bank balance calculated in (d) above be a debit or credit balance in Gold Ltd's accounting records?**

	✓
Debit	
Credit	

Task 2.2

On 28 June Kitchen Kuts received the following bank statement as at 23 June.

<table>
<tr><th colspan="5">Midway Bank PLC</th></tr>
<tr><th colspan="5">52 The Parade, Darton, DF10 9SW</th></tr>
<tr><td colspan="2">To: Kitchen Kuts</td><td>Account No 39103988</td><td colspan="2">23 June 20XX</td></tr>
<tr><th colspan="5">Statement of Account</th></tr>
<tr><td>Date</td><td>Detail</td><td>Paid out</td><td>Paid in</td><td>Balance</td></tr>
<tr><td>20XX</td><td></td><td>£</td><td>£</td><td>£</td></tr>
<tr><td>04 June</td><td>Balance b/f</td><td></td><td></td><td>15189</td><td>C</td></tr>
<tr><td>04 June</td><td>Cheque 111042</td><td>10,000</td><td></td><td>5,189</td><td>C</td></tr>
<tr><td>04 June</td><td>Cheque 111043</td><td>1,420</td><td></td><td>3,769</td><td>C</td></tr>
<tr><td>05 June</td><td>Cheque 111044</td><td>80</td><td></td><td>3,689</td><td>C</td></tr>
<tr><td>06 June</td><td>Cheque 111047</td><td>2,500</td><td></td><td>1,189</td><td>C</td></tr>
<tr><td>12 June</td><td>Bank Giro Credit Cabot & Co</td><td></td><td>571</td><td>1,760</td><td>C</td></tr>
<tr><td>13 June</td><td>Cheque 111045</td><td>795</td><td></td><td>965</td><td>C</td></tr>
<tr><td>13 June</td><td>Direct Debit LBMC</td><td>150</td><td></td><td>815</td><td>C</td></tr>
<tr><td>20 June</td><td>Direct Debit Insurance Direct</td><td>850</td><td></td><td>35</td><td>D</td></tr>
<tr><td>23 June</td><td>Bank Charges</td><td>88</td><td></td><td>123</td><td>D</td></tr>
<tr><td>23 June</td><td>Overdraft fee</td><td>30</td><td></td><td>153</td><td>D</td></tr>
<tr><td>23 June</td><td>Paid in at Midway Bank</td><td></td><td>175</td><td>22</td><td>C</td></tr>
<tr><td colspan="6" align="center">D = Debit   C = Credit</td></tr>
</table>

The cash book as at 23 June is shown below.

Cash book

Date 20XX	Details	Bank £	Date 20XX	Cheque number	Details	Bank £
01 June	Balance b/f	15,189	01 June	111042	Prime Kitchens	10,000
16 June	Britten & Bond	175	01 June	111043	Equipdirect	1,420
20 June	Macklin Ltd	950	01 June	111044	Long and Lane	80
21 June	Randle Fitments	300	01 June	111045	BLH Ltd	795
	▼		02 June	111046	MVR Ltd	652
	▼		02 June	111047	Fairfield Ltd	2,500
	▼		13 June	111048	Makin and King	450
	▼		13 June		LBMC	150
	▼				▼	
	▼				▼	
	▼				▼	
	▼				▼	
	▼				▼	

Picklist:

Balance b/d
Balance c/d
Bank charges
BLH Ltd
Britten & Bond
Cabot and Co
Closing balance
Equipdirect
Fairfield Ltd
Insurance Direct
LBMC
Long and Lane
Macklin Ltd
Makin and King
MVR Ltd
Opening balance
Overdraft fees
Prime Kitchens
Randle Fitments

(a) Check the items on the bank statement against the items in the cash book.

(b) Enter any items in the cash book as needed.

(c) Total the cash book and clearly show the balance carried down at 23 June (closing balance) and brought down at 24 June (opening balance).

(d) Complete the bank reconciliation statement as at 23 June.

Bank reconciliation statement as at 23 June 20XX

Balance per bank statement		£	
Add:			
Name:	▼	£	
Name:	▼	£	
Total to add		£	
Less:			
Name:	▼	£	
Name:	▼	£	
Total to subtract		£	
Balance as per cash book		£	

Picklist for line items:

Bank charges
BLH Ltd
Britten & Bond
Cabot and Co
Equipdirect
Fairfield Ltd
Insurance Direct
LBMC
Long and Lane
Macklin Ltd
Makin and King
MVR Ltd
Overdraft fees
Prime Kitchens
Randle Fitments

Task 2.3

This is a summary of petty cash payments made by Gold Ltd.

Entertaining   £35.90 (no VAT)
Window clearner paid   £25.00 (no VAT)
Emergency plumber paid £21.00 plus VAT

Use the relevant drag items below to:

(a) **Enter the above transactions in the petty cash book below**

(b) **Total the petty cash book and show the balance carried down**

Each drag item can be used more than once. You may not need to use all the drag items.

Petty cash book

Debit side		Credit side					
Details	Amount £	Details	Amount £	VAT £	Premises repairs £	Cleaning expenses £	Other operating costs £
Balance b/f	115.00	Entertaining					
		Window cleaner					
		Emergency plumber					
		Balance c/d					

Drag items:

4.20	30.00
5.00	33.10
7.18	35.90
16.38	43.08
16.72	81.90
21.00	86.10
25.00	98.28
25.20	115.00
28.90	

Task 2.4

At the end of June, the cash in the petty cash box was £29.99.

(a) **Complete the petty cash reimbursement document below to restore the imprest amount of £150.00 at 1 July.**

Petty cash reimbursement Date: 01.07,20XX Amount required to restore the cash in the petty cash box	£

Two receipts have now been handed in to the petty cashier.

Hales Service Station	
VAT registration number 297 3600 44	
3 July 20XX	
Fuel	£45.60
VAT at 20% is included in the above amount	
Gross amount	£38.00
VAT	£7.60
Paid cash	
Thank you for your custom	

PNM Office Supplies
VAT registration number 397 2896 35
6 July 20XX
5 boxes... plastic document wallets
@ £18.00 plus VAT @ 20%
£21.60 received in cash, thank you

(b) **Complete the petty cash vouchers below.**

Petty cash voucher		
Date: 3.07.XX		
Number: PC121		
Fuel		
Net	£	
VAT	£	
Gross	£	

Petty cash voucher		
Date: 6.07.XX		
Number: PC122		
Document wallets		
Net	£	
VAT	£	
Gross	£	

(c) **What is the new balance on the petty cash control account?**

£

The following notes and coins were in the petty cash box.

Notes and coins	£
6 × £10 notes	60.00
2 × £5 notes	10.00
16 × £1 coins	16.00
1 × 50p coins	0.50
11 × 20p coins	2.20
6 × 5p coins	0.30
20 × 1p coins	0.20

(d) **Complete the reconciliation below.**

The amount of cash in the petty cash box totals

£   which   ▼   reconcile with the balance on the petty cash control account.

Picklist:

does
does not

Task 2.5

This is a summary of transactions with suppliers during the month of June.

(a) **Show whether each entry will be a debit or credit in the purchases ledger control account in the general ledger.**

Details	Amount £	Debit ✓	Credit ✓
Balance of trade payables at 1 June	50,530		
Goods bought on credit	17,504		
Payments made to credit suppliers	20,672		
Discount received	392		
Goods returned to credit suppliers	784		

(b) **What will be the balance brought down on 1 July on the above account?**

	✓
Dr £ 54,874	
Cr £ 54,874	
Dr £ 46,970	
Cr £ 46,970	
Dr £ 46,186	
Cr £ 46,186	

The following credit balances were in the purchases ledger on 1 July.

	£
MMM Ltd	21,300
Walton Doors Ltd	4,198
Bramble and Barnet	123
Croxford and Company	15,530
Goodman Timber	1,119
Masefield Limited	3,524

(c) **Reconcile the balances shown above with the purchases ledger control account balance you have calculated in part (b).**

	£
Purchases ledger control account balance as at 30 June	
Total of purchases ledger accounts as at 30 June	
Difference	

(d) **What may have caused the difference you calculated in part (c)?**

	✓
Goods returned may have been omitted from the purchases ledger	
Discounts received may have been omitted from the purchases ledger	
Goods returned may have been entered in the purchases ledger twice	
Discounts received may have been entered in the purchases ledger twice	

It is important to reconcile the purchases ledger control account on a regular basis.

(e) **Which of the following statements is True?**

	✓
Reconciliation of the purchases ledger control account assures managers that the amount showing as outstanding from customers is correct	
Reconciliation of the purchases ledger control account assures managers that the amount showing as outstanding to suppliers is correct	
Reconciliation of the purchases ledger control account will show if a sales invoice has been omitted from the sales ledger	
Reconciliation of the purchases ledger control account will show if a sales invoice has been omitted from the purchases ledger	

Task 2.6

The following is an extract from Gold Ltd's books of prime entry.

Totals for quarter

Sales day book	**Purchases day book**
Net: £150,500	Net: £85,750
VAT: £30,100	VAT: £17,150
Gross:£180,600	Gross: £102,900

Sales returns day book	**Purchases returns day book**
Net: £2,450	Net: £6,650
VAT: £490	VAT: £1,330
Gross:£2,940	Gross: £7,980

Cash book

Net cash sales:	£280
VAT:	£56
Gross cash sales:	£336

(a) **What will be the entries in the VAT control account to record the VAT transactions in the quarter?**

Details		Amount £	Debit ✓	Credit ✓
	▼			
	▼			
	▼			
	▼			
	▼			

Picklist for line items:

Cash sales
Purchases
Purchases day book
Purchases returns
Purchases returns day book
Sales
Sales day book
Sales returns
Sales returns day book
VAT

The VAT return has been completed and shows an amount owing from HM Revenue and Customs of £13,846.

(b) **Is the VAT return correct?**

	✓
Yes	
No	

....

Task 2.7

Banks and building societies offer many similar services.

(a) **From the list below select TWO services that are NOT offered by building societies.**

Service	NOT offered by building societies ✓
Foreign currency	
Loan	
Overdraft	
Safe custody	
Savings account	
Telephone banking	

(b) **Show whether the following statements are True or False.**

	True ✓	False ✓
A bank cheque paid into a building society does not have to pass through the clearing system		
A building society cheque paid into a bank does not have to pass through the clearing system		
A bank cheque has to be passed to the bank of the issuer before the money becomes available		
A building society cheque has to be passed to the bank of the issuer before the money becomes available		

It is important to understand that banking documents need to be retained by an organisation so that accountants, HM Revenue and Customs and other organisations can access them when required.

(c) **Which TWO of the documents below are banking documents that must be retained by Kitchen Kuts?**

	✓
Aged trade receivables analysis	
Aged trade payables analysis	
Bank statements	
Credit cards	
Debit cards	
Paying in slip stubs	
Remittance advice notes	
Supplier invoices	

Task 2.8

Kitchen Kuts receives payment from customers and makes payments to suppliers in a variety of ways.

(a) **Select TWO checks that have to be made on each of the two payment methods shown below when received from customers.**

Checks to be made	Cheque ✓	Telephone credit card payment ✓
Check expiry date		
Check issue number		
Check not posted dated		
Check security number		
Check words and figures match		
Check card has not been tampered with		

BPP
LEARNING MEDIA

(b) **Show whether each of the statements below is True or False.**

	True ✓	False ✓
When Kitchen Kuts makes payments to suppliers by credit card, the amount leaves the bank current account immediately		
When Kitchen Kuts makes payments to suppliers by debit card, the amount paid does not affect the bank current account		

AAT PRACTICE ASSESSMENT 1
BASIC ACCOUNTING II

ANSWERS

Basic Accounting II AAT practice assessment 1

Section 1

Task 1.1

(a)

Account name	Amount £	Debit ✓	Credit ✓
Suspense	19,847	✓	

(b)

Error in the general ledger	Error disclosed by the trial balance ✓	Error NOT disclosed by the trial balance ✓
Recording a bank payment for heat and light on the debit side of both the bank and heat and light account	✓	
Recording a payment for motor repairs in the motor vehicles account		✓
Recording a sales credit note on the debit side of the sales ledger control account and the credit side of the sales returns account		✓
Incorrectly calculating the balance on the rent account	✓	
Recording a payment by cheque to a trade payable in the bank account and purchases ledger only	✓	
Recording a bank payment of £470 for motor repairs as £4,700 in both accounts		✓

Task 1.2

(a)

Account name	Amount £	Debit ✓	Credit ✓
Irrecoverable debts	1,680	✓	
VAT	336	✓	
Sales ledger control	2,016		✓

(b)

Account name	Amount £	Debit ✓	Credit ✓
Commission received	175		✓
Office equipment	1,555	✓	
Bank	368	✓	
Sales	3,500		✓
Capital	7,967		✓
Office expenses	876	✓	
Loan from bank	15,000		✓
Purchases	4,754	✓	
Motor vehicle	18,632	✓	
Motor vehicle expenses	457	✓	
Journal to record the opening entries of new business			

Task 1.3

(a)   Record the wages expense

Account name	Amount £	Debit ✓	Credit ✓
Wages expense	6,966	✓	
Wages control	6,966		✓

(b)   Record the HM Revenue and Customs liability

Account name	Amount £	Debit ✓	Credit ✓
HM Revenue and Customs	3,158		✓
Wages control	3,158	✓	

(c)   Record the wages paid to employees

Account name	Amount £	Debit ✓	Credit ✓
Bank	3,508		✓
Wages control	3,508	✓	

(d)   Record the Trade Union liability

Account name	Amount £	Debit ✓	Credit ✓
Trade Union	300		✓
Wages control	300	✓	

Task 1.4

(a)

(i)   Remove the incorrect entry

Account name	Amount £	Debit ✓	Credit ✓
VAT	2,400		✓

(ii)   Record the correct entry

Account name	Amount £	Debit ✓	Credit ✓
VAT	240	✓	

(iii)   Remove the suspense account balance

Account name	Amount £	Debit ✓	Credit ✓
Suspense	2,160	✓	

(b)

    (i)   Remove the incorrect entry

Account name	Amount £	Debit ✓	Credit ✓
Premises repairs	352	✓	
Bank	352		✓

    (ii)   Record the correct entry

Account name	Amount £	Debit ✓	Credit ✓
Premises repairs	352	✓	
Bank	352		✓

Task 1.5

Office stationery

Details	Amount £	Details	Amount £
Suspense	167		

Rent and rates

Details	Amount £	Details	Amount £
		Suspense	1,800

Suspense

Details	Amount £	Details	Amount £
Rent and rates	1,800	Balance b/f	1,633
		Office stationery	167

Bank interest received

Details	Amount £	Details	Amount £
Bank interest charged	98		

Bank interest charged

Details	Amount £	Details	Amount £
		Bank interest received	98

Task 1.6

	Balances extracted on 30 June £	Balances at 1 July	
		Debit £	Credit £
Motor vehicles	34,536	34,536	
Fixtures and fittings	17,350	17,350	
Inventory	7,300	7,300	
Bank overdraft	5,521	5,521	
Petty cash	100	100	
Sales ledger control	100,625	100,625	
Purchases ledger control	56,119		56,119
VAT owing to HM Revenue and Customs	8,300		8,300
Capital	22,844		22,844
Sales	222,955		222,955
Purchases	112,250	112,250	
Purchases returns	6,780		6,870
Wages	25,700	25,700	
Motor expenses	1,368	1,368	
Office expenses	3,354	3,354	
Rent and rates	1,444	1,444	
Heat and light	2,155	2,155	
Insurance	3,165	3,165	
Miscellaneous expenses	2,220	2,220	
Totals		317,088	317,088

Section 2

Task 2.1

(a)

Cash book – credit side

Details	Discount £	Cash £	Bank £	VAT £	Trade payables £	Cash purchases £	General repairs £
Balance b/f			1,150				
JBL Ltd		240		40		200	
Bocelli Brothers		336		56		280	
B and B Boards			376		376		
Rosen Ltd	38		1,890		1,890		
Bache Builders			1,128	188			940
Total	38	576	4,544	284	2,266	480	940

(b)

Cash book – debit side

Details	Discount £	Cash £	Bank £	Trade receivables £
Balance b/f		778		
Darren Davies			253	253
Clarkson Ltd	36		812	812
Total	36	778	1,065	1,065

(c) The correct answer is: £202 (778 – 576)

(d) The correct answer is: –£3,479 (1,065 – 4,544)

(e) The correct answer is: Credit balance

Task 2.2

(a) – (c)

Cash book

Date 20XX	Details	Bank £	Date 20XX	Cheque number	Details	Bank £
01 June	Balance b/f	15,189	01 June	111042	Prime Kitchens	10,000
16 June	Britten & Bond	175	01 June	111043	Equipdirect	1,420
20 June	Macklin Ltd	950	01 June	111044	Long and Lane	80
21 June	Randle Fitments	300	01 June	111045	BLH Ltd	795
12 June	Cabot and Co	571	02 June	111046	MVR Ltd	652
			02 June	111047	Fairfield Ltd	2,500
			13 June	111048	Makin and King	450
			13 June		LBMC	150
			20 June		Insurance Direct	850
			23 June		Bank charges	88
			23 June		Overdraft fees	30
			23 June		Balance c/d	170
		17,185				17,185
24 June	Balance b/d	170				

(d)

Bank reconciliation statement as at 23 June 20XX

Balance per bank statement		£	22
Add:			
Name:	Macklin Ltd	£	950
Name:	Randle Fitments	£	300
Total to add		£	1,250
Less:			
Name:	MVR Ltd	£	652
Name:	Makin and King	£	450
Total to subtract		£	1,102
Balance as per cash book		£	170

Task 2.3

(a) – (b)

Petty cash book

Debit side		Credit side					
Details	Amount £	Details	Amount £	VAT £	Premises repairs £	Cleaning expenses £	Other operating costs £
Balance b/f	115.00	Entertaining	35.90				35.90
		Window cleaner	25.00			25.00	
		Emergency plumber	25.20	4.20	21.00		
		Balance c/d	28.90				
	115.00		115.00	4.20	21.00	25.00	35.90

Task 2.4

(a) The correct answer is £120.01 (150.00 – 29.99)

(b)

Petty cash voucher		
Date: 3.07.XX		
Number: PC121		
Fuel		
Net	£	38.00
VAT	£	7.60
Gross	£	45.60

Petty cash voucher		
Date: 6.07.XX		
Number: PC122		
Document wallets		
Net	£	18.00
VAT	£	3.60
Gross	£	21.60

(c) The correct answer is £82.80 (150.00 – 45.60 – 21.60)

(d) The amount of cash in the petty cash box totals

£	89.20

which does not reconcile with the balance on the petty cash control account.

Task 2.5

(a)

Details	Amount £	Debit ✓	Credit ✓
Balance of trade payables at 1 June	50,530		✓
Goods bought on credit	17,504		✓
Payments made to credit suppliers	20,672	✓	
Discount received	392	✓	
Goods returned to credit suppliers	784	✓	

(b) The correct answer is: Credit £46,186
Working

	£
Balance of trade payables at 1 June	50,530
Goods bought on credit	17,504
Payments made to credit suppliers	(20,672)
Discount received	(392)
Goods returned to credit suppliers	(784)
Balance b/d 1 July	46,186

As this is the balance on the purchases ledger control account, it is a credit balance.

(c)

	£
Purchases ledger control account balance as at 30 June	46,186
Total of purchases ledger accounts as at 30 June	45,794
Difference	392

(d) The correct answer is: Discounts received may have been entered in the purchases ledger twice

The direction of the difference (purchases ledger total being less than the control account balance) could equally have been caused by entering discounts received twice or by entering goods returned twice in the purchases ledger, but the amount of the difference (£392) suggests that it is caused by discounts received of £392 being entered twice.

(e) The correct answer is: Reconciliation of the purchases ledger control account assures managers that the amount showing as outstanding to suppliers is correct

Task 2.6

(a)

Details	Amount £	Debit ✓	Credit ✓
Sales returns	490	✓	
Purchases	17,150	✓	
Sales	30,100		✓
Cash sales	56		✓
Purchases returns	1,330		✓

(b) The correct answer is: No

The amount is correct (30,100 + 56 + 1,330 – 490 – 17,150 = £13,846) but this is owed TO HMRC, not owing FROM them.

Task 2.7

(a) The correct answers are: Overdraft and Safe custody

Tutorial note: In fact many larger building societies do now offer this service

(b)

	True ✓	False ✓
A bank cheque paid into a building society does not have to pass through the clearing system		✓
A building society cheque paid into a bank does not have to pass through the clearing system		✓
A bank cheque has to be passed to the bank of the issuer before the money becomes available	✓	
A building society cheque has to be passed to the bank of the issuer before the money becomes available		✓

(c) The correct answers are: Bank statements and Paying in slip stubs

Task 2.8

(a)

Checks to be made	Cheque ✓	Telephone credit card payment ✓
Check expiry date		✓
Check issue number		
Check not posted dated	✓	
Check security number		✓
Check words and figures match	✓	
Check card has not been tampered with		

(b)

	True ✓	False ✓
When Kitchen Kuts makes payments to suppliers by credit card, the amount leaves the bank current account immediately		✓
When Kitchen Kuts makes payments to suppliers by debit card, the amount paid does not affect the bank current account		✓

AAT PRACTICE ASSESSMENT 2
BASIC ACCOUNTING II

Time allowed: 2 hours

Basic Accounting II AAT practice assessment 2

Section 1

Task 1.1

Gold Ltd's trial balance was extracted and did not balance. The debit column of the trial balance totalled £402,198 and the credit column totalled £403,536.

(a) **What entry would be made in the suspense account to balance the trial balance?**

Account name	Amount £	Debit ✓	Credit ✓
Suspense	1,338		

It is important to understand the types of errors than can occur within a double entry accounting system that will not be revealed by the trial balance.

(b) **Use the appropriate drag item below to match each of the descriptions with the type of error.**

Description of error	Type of error
An entry has been made in the sales ledger for the correct amount but the wrong customer's account has been used	
An entry has been made in the general ledger for the correct amount but the wrong type of account has been used, for example the office equipment account instead of the stationery account	
Debit and credit entries have been made in the correct accounts in the general ledger but for the wrong amount	
Debit and credit entries have been made in the correct accounts in the general ledger but on the wrong side of each account	
Errors have been made in the general ledger that cancel each other out, for example rent and rates have been overstated by £100 and electricity has been understated by £100	
No entries at all have been made in the general ledger for a transaction	

Drag items:

Compensating error

Error of commission

Error of omission

Error of original

Error of principle

Reversal of entries

Task 1.2

A credit customer, TL Jones, has ceased trading, owing Gold Ltd £8,016 **including** VAT.

(a) **Record the journal entries needed in the general ledger to write off the net amount and the VAT.**

Account name		Amount £	Debit ✓	Credit ✓
	▼			
	▼			
	▼			

Picklist:

Gold Ltd
Irrecoverable debts
Purchases
Purchases ledger control
Sales
Sales ledger control
TL Jones
VAT

Gold Ltd has started a new business, Glitz Ltd, and a new set of accounts is to be opened. A partially completed journal to record the opening entries is shown below.

(b) **Complete the journal by inserting each figure from the amount column in either the debit or credit column.**

The journal

Account name	Amount £	Debit £	Credit £
Bank overdraft	3,118		
Capital	12,500		
Cash sales	1,400		
Fixtures and fittings	4,320		
Heat and light	450		
Motor vehicle	8,700		
Purchases	6,478		
Purchases ledger control	3,650		
VAT on purchases	965		
VAT on sales	245		
Journal to record the opening entries of new business			

Task 1.3

Gold Ltd pays its employees by BACS transfer every month and maintains a wages control account. A summary of last month's payroll transactions is shown below.

Item	£
Gross wages	16,858
Income tax	4,012
Employer's NI	1,723
Employees' NI	1,446
Employees' pension contribution	900

Record the journal entries needed in the general ledger to:

(a) **Record the wages expense**

Account name	Amount £	Debit ✓	Credit ✓
▼			
▼			

(b) **Record the net wages paid to the employees**

Account name	Amount £	Debit ✓	Credit ✓
▼			
▼			

(c) **Record the HM Revenue and Customs liability**

Account name	Amount £	Debit ✓	Credit ✓
▼			
▼			

(d) **Record the pension liability**

Account name	Amount £	Debit ✓	Credit ✓
▼			
▼			

Picklist for line items:

Bank
Employees' NI
Employer's NI
HM Revenue and Customs
Income tax
Net wages
Pension
Wages control
Wages expense

Task 1.4

Gold Ltd's initial trial balance includes a suspense account.

The error has been traced to the entries made in the cash book and general ledger accounts on 4 June, as shown below.

Cash book – debit side

Date 200X	Details	Discounts £	Bank £
04 Jun	GHJ Ltd (credit customer)	146	4,275

Sales ledger control

Date 200X	Details	Amount £	Date 200X	Details	Amount £
			04 Jun	Bank	4,275
			04 Jun	Discount	146

Discounts received

Date 200X	Details	Amount £	Date 200X	Details	Amount £
			04 Jun	Sales ledger control	146

(a) **Identify the error and record the journal entries needed in the general ledger to:**

   (i) **Remove the incorrect entry**

Account name	Amount £	Debit ✓	Credit ✓
▼			

   (ii) **Record the correct entry**

Account name	Amount £	Debit ✓	Credit ✓
▼			

(iii) **Remove the suspense account balance**

Account name		Amount £	Debit ✓	Credit ✓
▼				

Picklist for line items:

Bank
Cash
Discounts allowed
Discounts received
Purchases ledger control
Sales ledger control
Suspense

An entry to record a cheque for £95, received in respect of a refund of rent paid, had been reversed.

(b) **Record the journal entries needed in the general ledger to:**

(i) **Remove the incorrect entry**

Account name		Amount £	Debit ✓	Credit ✓
▼				
▼				

(ii) **Record the correct entry**

Account name		Amount £	Debit ✓	Credit ✓
▼				
▼				

Picklist for line items:

Bank
Cash
Purchases ledger control
Rent paid
Rent received
Sales ledger control
Suspense

Task 1.5

Gold Ltd's initial trial balance included a suspense account. All of the bookkeeping errors have now been traced and the journal entries shown below have been recorded.

Journal entries

Account Name	Debit £	Credit £
Fixtures and fittings	3,117	
Office equipment		3,117
Office expenses	248	
Suspense		248
Suspense	816	
Legal fees		816

Use the relevant drag items below to post the journal entries to the general ledger accounts.

Fixtures and fittings

Details	Amount £	Details	Amount £

Office equipment

Details	Amount £	Details	Amount £

Office expenses

Details	Amount £	Details	Amount £

Drag items:

Fixtures and fittings

Legal fees

Office equipment

Office expenses

Suspense

Suspense

248

Suspense

Details	Amount £	Details	Amount £
		Balance b/f	568

248

816

Legal fees

Details	Amount £	Details	Amount £

816

3,117

3,117

Task 1.6

On 30 June, Gold Ltd extracted an initial trial balance which did not balance, and a suspense account was opened with an £800 credit balance. On 1 July, three journal entries were prepared to correct the errors that had been found, and clear the suspense account. The journal entries to correct the errors, and the list of balances in the initial trial balance, are shown below.

Re-draft the trial balance by placing the figures in the debit or credit column. You should take into account the journal entries which will clear the suspense account. Do not enter figures with decimal places in this task.

Journal entries

Account name	Debit £	Credit £
Wages and salaries	790	
Office expenses		790

Account name	Debit £	Credit £
Suspense	1,434	
Rent received		1,434

Account name	Debit £	Credit £
Motor expenses	634	
Suspense		634

Trial balance

Account name	Balances extracted on 30 June £	Debit balances at 1 July £	Credit balances at 1 July £
Accountant's fees	1,850		
Irrecoverable debts written off	2,150		
Bank overdraft	956		
Capital	17,885		
Discounts allowed	329		
Miscellaneous expenses	1,297		
Motor expenses	2,235		
Office expenses	1,723		
Petty cash	200		
Purchases	87,013		
Purchases ledger control	50,324		
Purchases returns	1,528		
Rent received	3,600		
Sales	171,400		
Sales ledger control	102,644		
Sales returns	2,100		
Travel expenses	3,269		
VAT owing from HM Revenue and Customs	2,433		
Wages and salaries	39,250		
Totals			

Section 2

Task 2.1

There are four payments to be entered in Gold Ltd's cash book:

Payments to suppliers who do not offer credit accounts:

- Cash paid to Henry Hughes of £192, including VAT, for goods purchased.

- A bank payment of £570, no VAT, to BGH Insurance.

Payments to credit suppliers:

- BACS payments made as authorised on the two invoices shown below.

Fraser plc	
5 Tyson Road, Darton, DF6 9HY	
VAT Registration No. 217 6421 00	
Invoice No. 239	30 June 20XX
To: Gold Ltd	
14 High Street,	
Darton, DF11 4GX	
	£
800 items of FZ @ £0.50 each	400.00
VAT @ 20%	72.00
Total	472.00
Authorised for payment of £432, £40 settlement discount taken: J Cook	
Terms: 10% settlement discount for payment in 10 days or 30 days net	

H. Bains	
27 Head Street, Darton, DF7 5ND	
VAT Registration No. 391 7429 00	
Invoice No. X77	30 June 20
To: Gold Ltd	
14 High Street,	
Darton, DF11 4GX	
	£
96 items of JV @ £2.50 each	240.00
VAT @ 20%	48.00
Total	288.00
Authorised for payment in full: J Cook	
Terms: 30 days net	

(a) **Enter the details of the four payments into the credit side of the cash book shown below and total each column.**

Cash book – credit side

Details	Discount £	Cash £	Bank £	VAT £	Trade payables £	Cash purchases £	Insurance £
Balance b/f			1,216				
Total							

There are three amounts received to be entered in Gold Ltd's cash book.

Cheques received from credit customers:

- FH Castings £1,149
- Tobyn plc £1,590 (this customer has taken a £60 settlement discount)

Cash received:

- £130 received from Jane Clifton for rent of office space. (Ignore VAT)

(b) **Enter the above details into the debit side of the cash-book and total each column.**

Cash book – debit side

Details	Discount £	Cash £	Bank £	Trade receivables £	Other operating income £
Balance b/f		327			
Total					

Picklist for line items:

BGH Insurance
FH Casting
Fraser plc
H Bains
Henry Hughes
Jane Clifton
Tobyn plc

(c) **Using your answers to (a) and (b) above, calculate the cash balance. Do not use commas when entering figures in this part of the question.**

£ [   ]

(d) **Using your answers to (a) and (b) above, calculate the bank balance. If your calculations show that the bank account is overdrawn your answer should start with a minus sign, for example –123. Do not use commas when entering figures in this part of the question.**

£ [   ]

(e) **What will be the entry in Fraser's plc account in the purchases ledger to record the discount received?**

Purchases ledger

Account name	Amount £	Debit ✓	Credit ✓
Fraser plc			

BPP
LEARNING MEDIA

Task 2.2

On 28 July, Gold Ltd received the following bank statements as at 27 July.

MIDWAY BANK plc

52 The Parade, Darton, DF10 9SW

To: Gold Ltd   Account No 39103988   27 July 20XX

Statement of Account

Date 200X	Detail	Paid out £	Paid in £	Balance £
01 July	Balance b/f			3,034 D
01 July	BACS transfer – Tully Traders		3,712	
01 July	Cheque 001399	126		
01 July	Direct Debit – PCL Ltd	1,812		1,260 D
04 July	Counter credit		1,200	60 D
12 July	Cheque 001400	320		380 D
22 July	CHAPS transfer – Legal institute		50,000	49,620 C
22 July	Standing order – WVC Ltd	525		49,095 C
27 July	Bank charges	89		
27 July	Cheque 001402	2,218		46,788 C

D = Debit   C = Credit

The cash book as at 27 July is shown below.

Cash book

Date 20XX	Details	Bank £	Date 20XX	Cheque Number	Details	Bank £
01 Jul	Balance b/f	552	01 Jul	001400	Barnes Builders	320
01 Jul	D Clements	1,200	02 Jul	001401	C Smithson	1,500
04 Jul	Paxo Partners	4,124	08 Jul	001402	Boyd Brothers	2,218
20 Jul	Johnson plc	1,688	12 Jul	001403	Corser Ltd	85

(a) **Check the items on the bank statement against the items in the cash book.**

(b) **Enter any items in the cash book as needed.**

(c) **Total the cash book and clearly show the balance carried down at 27 July AND brought down at 28 July.**

(d) **Complete the bank reconciliation statement as at 27 July.**

Balance per bank statement	£
Add:	
Name:	£
Name:	£
Total to add	£
Less:	
Name:	£
Name:	£
Total to subtract	£
Balance as per cash book	£

Picklist for line items:

Balance b/d
Balance c/d
Bank charges
Barnes Builders
Boyd Brothers
C Smithson
Cheque 001399
Corser Ltd
D Clements
Johnson plc
Legal Institute
Paxo Partners
PCL Ltd
Tully Traders
WVC Ltd

··

Task 2.3

This is a summary of petty cash payments made by Gold Ltd during one week.

- Tea/coffee paid £9.60 (no VAT)

- Printer paper purchased £16.80 plus VAT

- Rail fare paid £27.20 (no VAT)

Use the relevant drag items below to:

(a) **Enter the above transactions in the petty cash book below**

(b) **Total the petty cash book and show the balance carried down**

Each drag item can be used more than once. You may not need to use all of the drag items.

Petty cash book

Debit side		Credit side					
Details	Amount £	Details	Amount £	VAT £	Office expenses £	Travel expenses £	General expenses £
Balance b/f	100.00	Tea/coffee					
		Printer paper					
		Rail fare					
		Balance c/d					

Drag items:

100.00	64.32	56.96	53.60	46.40	43.04	35.68	32.64	27.20

20.16	16.80	11.52	10.72	9.60	5.44	3.36	1.92

Task 2.4

Gold Ltd operates a petty cash system with an imprest amount of £200.

On 1 July, the cash in the petty box was £39.47.

(a) **Complete the petty cash reimbursement document below to restore the imprest amount.**

Petty cash reimbursement	
Date: 1.07.20XX	
Amount required to restore the cash in the petty cash box	£

On 4 July the following receipt was presented for payment from petty cash.

Grays Garage
Cash receipt 089
Date: 04.07.20XX
Cash received for the purchasing of motor fuel, £30.72 including VAT.
Jane Gray

(b) **Complete the petty cash voucher below.**

Petty cash voucher	
Date: 04.07.20XX	Number: PC227

Motor fuel		
Net	£	
VAT	£	
Gross	£	

By 31 July further amounts totalling £103.49 had been paid from petty cash.

(c) **What is the balance on the petty cash account on 31 July?**

£

The cash in the petty cash box on 3 July was checked and the notes and coins in the table below were there.

(d) **Insert the missing figures to complete the table and show the total amount in the petty cash box.**

Notes and coins	£
2 × £10 notes	20.00
5 × £5 notes	25.00
3 × £2 coins	6.00
7 × £1 coins	7.00
7 × 50p coins	3.50
8 × 20p coins	
9 × 5p coins	
11 × 2p coins	
TOTAL	

(e) **What is the difference between the balance on the petty cash account and the total amount of cash in the petty cash box on 31 July?**

£

....

Task 2.5

At the end of June, the purchases ledger control account had debit entries amounting to £25,296 and credit entries amounting to £96,735.

(a) **What will be the balance on the purchases ledger control account?**

£

(b) **Will the balance you calculated in (a) be a debit or credit balance brought down in the purchases ledger control account?**

▼

Picklist:

Debit
Credit

The following balances were in the purchases ledger at the end of June.

Purchases ledger accounts	£
PBR Ltd	22,392
Morton plc	1,900
Axion & Co	11,363
Barford Builders	33,225
Jonty & Co	4,600
Pendeford Paints	659

(c) **Which one of the statements below is True?**

	✓
The purchases ledger control account balance matches the total of the balances in the purchases ledger so no further action is necessary	
The purchases ledger control account balance does not match the total of the balances in the purchases ledger so the difference must be investigated.	
It is not important that the balance of the purchases ledger control account matches the total of the balances in the purchases ledger so no further action is necessary	

This is a summary of transactions with credit suppliers during the month of July.

(d) **Show whether each entry will be a debit or credit in the purchases ledger control account in the general ledger.**

Purchases ledger control

Details	Amount £	Debit ✓	Credit ✓
Purchases from credit suppliers	36,421		
Payments made to credit suppliers	18,760		
Discounts received	1,225		
Goods returned to credit suppliers	2,460		

This is a summary of transactions with credit customers during the month of July.

(e) **Show whether each entry will be a debit or credit in the sales ledger control account in the general ledger.**

Sales ledger control

Details	Amount £	Debit ✓	Credit ✓
Discounts allowed	850		
Goods sold on credit	60,151		
Goods returned by credit customers	745		
Irrecoverable debts written off	900		

Task 2.6

During the last VAT quarter, a VAT refund of £17,168 was received by BACS transfer.

(a) **What would have been the entries in the general ledger to record this refund?**

Account name		Amount £	Debit ✓	Credit ✓
	▼			
	▼			

Picklist:

BACS
Bank
Cash
VAT control

At the end of the last VAT quarter, the VAT control account had debit entries amounting to £56,189 and credit entries amounting to £88,233.

(b) **What will be the balance in the VAT control account?**

£

(c) **Will the balance you calculated in (b) be a debit or credit balance brought down in the VAT control account?**

▼

Picklist:

Debit
Credit

This is a summary of VAT transactions during the current VAT quarter.

(d) **Show whether each entry will be a debit or credit in the VAT control account in the general ledger.**

Summary of VAT transactions

Details	Amount £	Debit ✓	Credit ✓
VAT recorded in purchases day book	26,324		
VAT recorded in purchases returns day book	276		
VAT recorded in sales day book	38,172		
VAT recorded in sales returns day book	345		
VAT recorded in cash book from cash sales	1,360		
VAT recorded in cash book from cash purchases	2,188		
VAT recorded in petty cash book	76		
Journal to record the VAT amount of an irrecoverable debt written off	215		

Task 2.7

Banks offer a variety of services to customers including bank overdrafts, bank drafts, bank loans and BACS.

(a) **Use the drag items below to match each service to the most appropriate service description. You can only use each drag item once.**

Service description	Service
A method of distributing cheques	
A method of making direct payments	
A method of storing cash	
A cheque issued by a bank	
A cheque issued by a customer	
An uncrossed cheque	
A method of borrowing money on a short term basis	
A method of borrowing money on a long term basis	
A method of borrowing money on an interest free basis	
A method of borrowing money from your employer	

Drag items:

Bank overdraft

Bank draft

Bank loan

BACS

Small mutual building societies usually offer fewer services than banks.

(b) **Select FOUR services most likely to be offered by small mutual building societies from the list below.**

Services	✓
Foreign currency	
Corporate credit cards	
Savings accounts	
Insurance services	
Bookkeeping service	
Mortgages	
Business current accounts	
Safe custody	

Task 2.8

Gold Ltd receives payments from customers in different ways. One method often used is credit card payment by telephone.

(a) **Select THREE questions Gold Ltd should ask when accepting a credit card payment by telephone.**

Questions	✓
What is the issue number?	
What is the credit limit?	
What is the security number?	
What is the expiry date?	
What is the PIN?	
What is the name that appears on the card?	

(b) **Show whether the following statement is True or False.**

Statement	True ✓	False ✓
It is possible to make payments by telephone using a debit card.		

(c) **Select TWO checks that Gold Ltd should make when a cheque is received from a customer.**

Checks	✓
Check the customer's account in the purchases ledger.	
Check the bank statement.	
Check the date on the cheque.	
Check the funds are available in the customer's bank account	
Check the amount on the cheque in words and figures.	

AAT PRACTICE ASSESSMENT 2
BASIC ACCOUNTING II

ANSWERS

Basic Accounting II AAT practice assessment 2

Section 1

Task 1.1

(a)

Account name	Amount £	Debit ✓	Credit ✓
Suspense	1,338	✓	

(b)

Description of error	Type of error
An entry has been made in the sales ledger for the correct amount but the wrong customer's account has been used	Error of commission
An entry has been made in the general ledger for the correct amount but the wrong type of account has been used, for example the office equipment account instead of the stationery account	Error of principle
Debit and credit entries have been made in the correct accounts in the general ledger but for the wrong amount	Error of original entry
Debit and credit entries have been made in the correct accounts in the general ledger but on the wrong side of each account	Reversal of entries
Errors have been made in the general ledger that cancel each other out, for example rent and rates have been overstated by £100 and electricity has been understated by £100	Compensating error
No entries at all have been made in the general ledger for a transaction	Error of omission

Task 1.2

(a)

Account name	Amount £	Debit ✓	Credit ✓
Irrecoverable debts	6,680	✓	
VAT	1,336	✓	
Sales ledger control	8,016		✓

(b) **The journal**

Account name	Amount £	Debit £	Credit £
Bank overdraft	3,118		3,118
Capital	12,500		12,500
Cash sales	1,400		1,400
Fixtures and fittings	4,320	4,320	
Heat and light	450	450	
Motor vehicle	8,700	8,700	
Purchases	6,478	6,478	
Purchases ledger control	3,650		3,650
VAT on purchases	965	965	
VAT on sales	245		245
Journal to record the opening entries of new business			

Task 1.3

(a) Record the wages expense

Account name	Amount £	Debit ✓	Credit ✓
Wages expense	18,581	✓	
Wages control	18,581		✓

(b) Record the net wages paid to employee

Account name	Amount £	Debit ✓	Credit ✓
Wages control	10,500	✓	
Bank	10,500		✓

(c) Record the HM Revenue and Customs liability

Account name	Amount £	Debit ✓	Credit ✓
Wages control	7,181	✓	
HM Revenue and Customs	7,181		✓

(d) Record the pension liability

Account name	Amount £	Debit ✓	Credit ✓
Wages control	900	✓	
Pension	900		✓

· ·

Task 1.4

(a) (i) Remove the incorrect entry

Account name	Amount £	Debit ✓	Credit ✓
Discounts received	146	✓	

(ii) Record the correct entry

Account name	Amount £	Debit ✓	Credit ✓
Discounts allowed	146	✓	

(iii) Remove the suspense account balance

Account name	Amount £	Debit ✓	Credit ✓
Suspense	292		✓

(b) (i) Remove the incorrect entry

Account name	Amount £	Debit ✓	Credit ✓
Bank	95	✓	
Rent paid	95		✓

(ii) Record the correct entry

Account name	Amount £	Debit ✓	Credit ✓
Bank	95	✓	
Rent paid	95		✓

Task 1.5

Fixtures and fittings

Details	Amount £	Details	Amount £
Office equipment	3,117		

Office equipment

Details	Amount	Details	Amount
	£		£
		Fixtures and fittings	3,117

Office expenses

Details	Amount	Details	Amount
	£		£
Suspense	248		

Suspense

Details	Amount	Details	Amount
	£		£
Legal fees	816	Balance b/f	568
		Office expenses	248

Legal fees

Details	Amount	Details	Amount
	£		£
		Suspense	816

Task 1.6

Trial balance

Account name	Balances extracted on 30 June £	Debit balances at 1 July £	Credit balances at 1 July £
Accountant's fees	1,850	1,850	
Irrecoverable debts written off	2,150	2,150	
Bank overdraft	956		956
Capital	17,885		17,885
Discounts allowed	329	329	
Miscellaneous expenses	1,297	1,297	
Motor expenses	2,235	2,869	
Office expenses	1,723	933	
Petty cash	200	200	
Purchases	87,013	87,013	
Purchases ledger control	50,324		50,324
Purchases returns	1,528		1,528
Rent received	3,600		5,034
Sales	171,400		171,400
Sales ledger control	102,644	102,644	
Sales returns	2,100	2,100	
Travel expenses	3,269	3,269	
VAT owing from HM Revenue and Customs	2,433	2,433	
Wages and salaries	39,250	40,040	
Totals		**247,127**	**247,127**

Section 2

Task 2.1

(a)

Cash book – credit side

Details	Discount £	Cash £	Bank £	VAT £	Trade payables £	Cash purchases £	Insurance £
Balance b/f			1,216				
Henry Hughes		192		32		160	
BGH Insurance			570				570
Fraser plc	40		432		432		
H Bains			288		288		
Total	40	192	2,506	32	720	160	570

(b)

Cash book – debit side

Details	Discount £	Cash £	Bank £	Trade receivables £	Other operating income £
Balance b/f		327			
FH Castings			1,149	1,149	
Tobyn plc	60		1,590	1,590	
Jane Clifton		130			130
Total	60	457	2,739	2,739	130

(c) The correct answer is: £265 (457 – 192 = 265)

(d) The correct answer is: £233 (2,739 – 2,506 = 233)

(e)

Purchases ledger

Account name	Amount £	Debit ✓	Credit ✓
Fraser plc	40	✓	

Task 2.2

(a) – (c)

Cash book

Date 20XX	Details	Bank £	Date 20XX	Cheque Number	Details	Ba £
01 Jul	Balance b/f	552	01 Jul	001400	Barnes Builders	3
01 Jul	D Clements	1,200	02 Jul	001401	C Smithson	1,5
04 Jul	Paxo Partners	4,124	08 Jul	001402	Boyd Brothers	2,2
20 Jul	Johnson plc	1,688	12 Jul	001403	Corser Ltd	
22 Jul	Legal Institute	50,000	1 Jul		PCL Ltd	1,8
			22 Jul		WVC Ltd	5
			27 Jul		Bank charges	
			27 Jul		Balance c/d	51,0
		57,564				57,5
28 Jul	Balance c/d	51,015				

(d)

Balance per bank statement	£ 46,788
Add:	
Name: Paxo Partners	£ 4,124
Name: Johnson plc	£ 1,688
Total to add	£ 5,812
Less:	
Name: C Smithson	£ 1,500
Name: Corser Ltd	£ 85
Total to subtract	£ 1,585
Balance as per cash book	£ 51,015

Task 2.3

Petty cash book

Debit Side		Credit side					
Details	Amount	Details	Amount £	VAT £	Office expenses £	Travel expenses £	General expenses £
Balance b/f	100.00	Tea/coffee	9.60				9.60
		Printer paper	20.16	3.36	16.80		
		Rail fare	27.20			27.20	
		Balance c/d	43.04				
	100.00		100.00	3.36	16.80	27.20	9.60

Task 2.4

(a)

Petty cash reimbursement	
Date: 1.07.20XX	
Amount required to restore the cash in the petty cash box	£ 160.53

Working

£200 – £39.47 = £160.53

(b)

Petty cash voucher	
Date: 04.07.20XX	Number: PC227
Motor fuel	
Net	£
VAT	£
Gross	£

(c)   The correct answer is: £65.79 (£200 – £30.72 – £103.49 = £65.79)

(d)

Notes and coins	£
2 × £10 notes	20.00
5 × £5 notes	25.00
3 × £2 coins	6.00
7 × £1 coins	7.00
7 × 50p coins	3.50
8 × 20p coins	1.60
9 × 5p coins	0.45
11 × 2p coins	0.22
TOTAL	63.77

(e) The correct answer is: £2.02 (65.79 – 63.77 = 2.02)

Task 2.5

(a) The correct answer is: £71,439 (96,735 – 25,296 = 71,439)

(b) The correct answer is: Credit

(c) The correct answer is: Purchases ledger control account balance does not match the total of the balances in the purchases ledger so the difference must be investigated

(d)

Purchases ledger control

Details	Amount £	Debit ✓	Credit ✓
Purchases from credit suppliers	36,421		✓
Payments made to credit suppliers	18,760	✓	
Discounts received	1,225	✓	
Goods returned to credit suppliers	2,460	✓	

(e)

Sales ledger control

Details	Amount £	Debit ✓	Credit ✓
Discounts allowed	850		✓
Goods sold on credit	60,151	✓	
Goods returned by credit customers	745		✓
Irrecoverable debts written off	900		✓

Task 2.6

(a)

Account name	Amount £	Debit ✓	Credit ✓
Bank	17,168	✓	
VAT control	17,168		✓

(b)　The correct answer is: £32,044 (88,233 – 56,189 = 32,044)

(c)　The correct answer is: Credit

(d)　**Summary of VAT transactions**

Details	Amount £	Debit ✓	Credit ✓
VAT recorded in purchases day-book	26,324	✓	
VAT recorded in purchases returns day-book	276		✓
VAT recorded in sales day-book	38,172		✓
VAT recorded in sales returns day-book	345	✓	
VAT recorded in cash-book from cash sales	1,360		✓
VAT recorded in cash-book from cash purchases	2,188	✓	
VAT recorded in petty cash-book	76	✓	
Journal to record the VAT amount of an irrecoverable debt written off	215	✓	

Task 2.7

(a)

Service description	Service
A method of distributing cheques	
A method of making direct payments	BACS
A method of storing cash	
A cheque issued by a bank	Bank draft
A cheque issued by a customer	
An uncrossed cheque	
A method of borrowing money on a short term basis	Bank overdraft
A method of borrowing money on a long term basis	Bank loan
A method of borrowing money on an interest free basis	
A method of borrowing money from your employer	

(b)

Services	✓
Foreign currency	✓
Corporate credit cards	
Savings accounts	✓
Insurance services	✓
Bookkeeping service	
Mortgages	✓
Business current accounts	
Safe custody	

Task 2.8

(a)

Questions	✓
What is the issue number?	
What is the credit limit?	
What is the security number?	✓
What is the expiry date?	✓
What is the PIN?	
What is the name that appears on the card?	✓

(b)

Statement	True	False
It is possible to make payments by telephone using a debit card.	✓	

(c)

Checks	✓
Check the customer's account in the purchases ledger.	
Check the bank statement.	
Check the date on the cheque.	✓
Check the funds are available in the customer's bank account	
Check the amount on the cheque in words and figures.	✓

BPP PRACTICE ASSESSMENT 1
BASIC ACCOUNTING II

Time allowed: 2 hours

Basic Accounting II BPP practice assessment 1

Section 1

Task 1.1

Russell Hardware's trial balance was extracted and did not balance. The debit column of the trial balance totalled £297,564 and the credit column totalled £295,128.

(a) **What entry would be made in the suspense account to balance the trial balance?**

Account name	Amount £	Debit ✓	Credit ✓
Suspense			

It is important to understand the types of error that are disclosed by the trial balance and those that are not.

(b) **Show which of the errors below are, or are not, disclosed by the trial balance.**

Error in the general ledger	Error disclosed by the trial balance ✓	Error NOT disclosed by the trial balance ✓
Writing in the balance on the office stationery account incorrectly		
Recording a purchase from a credit supplier for £5,000 (no VAT) as £500 in both the purchases and the purchases ledger control accounts		
Recording a receipt from a credit customer in the cash sales account		
Recording a credit note from a supplier on the debit side of the purchases ledger control account and the debit side of the purchases returns account		
Recording a bank receipt from a customer on the credit side of both the bank and the sales ledger control account		
Recording a receipt from a credit customer in the bank account and sales ledger control account only		

Task 1.2

A credit customer, Jensen Ltd, has ceased trading, owing Russell Hardware £1,120 plus VAT.

(a) **Record the journal entries needed in the general ledger to write off the net amount and the VAT.**

Account name		Amount £	Debit ✓	Credit ✓
	▼			
	▼			
	▼			

Picklist for line items:

Irrecoverable debts
Jensen Ltd
Russell Hardware
Purchases
Purchases ledger control
Sales
Sales ledger control
VAT

(b) Russell Hardware has started a new business, Russell Giftware, and a new set of accounts is to be opened. A partially completed journal to record the opening balances is shown below.

Record the journal entries needed in the accounts in the general ledger of Russell Giftware to deal with the opening balances.

Account name	Amount £	Debit ✓	Credit ✓
Capital	10,000		
Cash at bank	2,500		
Computer	750		
Furniture and fittings	950		
Heat and light	100		
Loan from bank	5,000		
Office expenses	320		
Petty cash	200		
Purchases	9,680		
Rent and rates	500		
Journal to record the opening entries of new business			

Task 1.3

Russell Hardware pays its employees by cheque every month and maintains a wages control account. A summary of last month's payroll transactions is shown below:

Item	£
Gross wages	7,450
Employees' NI	682
Income tax	1,204
Employees' pension contributions	90
Employer's NI	809

Record the journal entries needed in the general ledger to:

(a) **Record the wages expense**

Account name	Amount £	Debit ✓	Credit ✓
▼			
▼			

(b) **Record the HM Revenue and Customs liability**

Account name	Amount £	Debit ✓	Credit ✓
▼			
▼			

(c) **Record the net wages paid to the employees**

Account name	Amount £	Debit ✓	Credit ✓
▼			
▼			

(d) **Record the pension administrator liability**

Account name	Amount £	Debit ✓	Credit ✓
▼			
▼			

Picklist:

Bank
Employees' NI
Employer's NI
HM Revenue and Customs
Income tax
Net wages
Pension administrator
Wages control
Wages expense

Task 1.4

Russell Hardware's initial trial balance includes a suspense account with a balance of £396.

The error has been traced to the purchases day book shown below.

Purchases day book

Date 20XX	Details	Invoice number	Total £	VAT £	Net £
30 Jun	Fixit Ltd	8932	6,000	1,000	5,000
30 Jun	Frame Products Ltd	1092	912	152	760
30 Jun	SDF plc	663	1,536	256	1,280
	Totals		8,844	1,408	7,040

(a) **Identify the error and record the journal entries needed in the general ledger to**

(i) **Remove the incorrect entry**

Account name	Amount £	Debit ✓	Credit ✓
▼			

(ii) **Record the correct entry**

Account name	Amount £	Debit ✓	Credit ✓
▼			

(iii) **Remove the suspense account balance**

Account name	Amount £	Debit ✓	Credit ✓
▼			

Picklist:

Fixit Ltd
Frame Products Ltd
SDF plc
Purchases
Purchases day book
Purchases ledger control
Purchases returns
Purchases returns day book
Sales
Sales day book
Sales ledger control
Sales returns
Sales returns day book
Suspense
VAT

An entry to record a bank receipt of £1,400 from a credit customer has been reversed.

(b) **Record the journal entries needed in the general ledger to**

(i) **Remove the incorrect entries**

Account name		Amount £	Debit ✓	Credit ✓
	▼			
	▼			

(ii) **Record the correct entries**

Account name		Amount £	Debit ✓	Credit ✓
	▼			
	▼			

Picklist for line items:

Bank
Cash
Purchases
Purchases ledger control
Sales
Sales ledger control
Suspense
VAT

Task 1.5

Russell Hardware's trial balance included a suspense account. All the bookkeeping errors have now been traced and the journal entries shown below have been recorded.

Journal entries

Account name	Debit £	Credit £
Irrecoverable debts	73	
Suspense		73
Heat and light	150	
Office expenses		150
Suspense	201	
Marketing expenses		201

Post the journal entries to the general ledger accounts. Dates are not required.

Irrecoverable debts

Details	Amount £	Details	Amount £
▼			
▼			
▼			

Heat and light

Details	Amount £	Details	Amount £
▼			
▼			
▼			

Marketing expenses

Details	Amount £	Details	Amount £
▼			
▼			
▼			

Office expenses

Details	Amount £	Details	Amount £
▼			
▼			
▼			

Suspense

Details	Amount £	Details	Amount £
		Balance b/f	128
▼			
▼			

Picklist for line items:

Balance b/d
Irrecoverable debts
Heat and light
Marketing expenses
Office expenses
Suspense

Task 1.6

On 30 June Russell Hardware extracted an initial trial balance which did not balance, and a suspense account was opened. On 1 July journal entries were prepared to correct the errors that had been found, and clear the suspense account. The list of balances in the initial trial balance, and the journal entries to correct the errors, are shown below. The list of balances has not yet been updated for the journal entries.

BPP
LEARNING MEDIA

Taking into account the journal entries, which will clear the suspense account, re-draft the trial balance by placing the figures in the debit or credit column.

	Balances extracted on 30 June £	Balances at 1 July	
		Debit £	Credit £
Motor vehicles	13,920		
Furniture and fittings	9,208		
Inventory	10,129		
Cash at bank	673		
Petty cash	250		
Sales ledger control	7,832		
Purchases ledger control	4,292		
VAT owing to HM Revenue and Customs	1,029		
Capital	10,000		
Sales	89,125		
Purchases	35,268		
Purchases returns	1,092		
Wages	18,279		
Marketing expenses	1,290		
Office expenses	3,287		
Rent and rates	2,819		
Heat and light	1,056		
Irrecoverable debts	127		
Motor expenses	1,820		
Suspense (credit balance)	420		
Totals			

Journal entries

Account name	Debit £	Credit £
Purchases ledger control		507
Suspense	507	
Purchases ledger control		507
Suspense	507	

Account name	Debit £	Credit £
Heat and light		1,056
Suspense	1,056	
Heat and light	1,650	
Suspense		1,650

Section 2

Task 2.1

Russell Hardware has made five payments which are to be entered in its cash book.

Receipts for payments

| Received cash with thanks for goods bought.

From Russell Hardware, a customer without a credit account.

Net £40
VAT £8
Total £48

Cranula Ltd | Received cash with thanks for goods bought.

From Russell Hardware, a customer without a credit account.

Net £240
VAT £48
Total £288

Gesteor & Co | Received cash with thanks for goods bought.

From Russell Hardware, a customer without a credit account.

Net £167
(No VAT)

S Ransome |

Cheque book counterfoils

| Weston Ltd
(Purchase ledger account WES001)

£1,452
(Note: Have taken £30 settlement discount)

109923 | Stationery Shop Ltd
(We have no credit account with this supplier)

£240 including VAT

109924 |

(a) **Enter the details from the three receipts and two cheque book stubs into the credit side of the cash book shown below and total each column.**

Cash book – credit side

Details	Discount £	Cash £	Bank £	VAT £	Purchases ledger £	Cash purchases £	Stationery £
Balance b/f			135				
Cranula Ltd							
Gesteor & Co							
S Ransome							
Weston Ltd							
Stationery Shop Ltd							
Total							

There are also two cheques from credit customers to be entered in Russell Hardware's cash book:

Middle Firth Ltd £673

High Tops plc £1,092 (this customer has taken a £50 discount)

(b) **Enter the above details into the debit side of the cash book and total each column.**

Cash book – debit side

Details	Discount £	Cash £	Bank £	Sales ledger £
Balance b/f		629		
Middle Firth Ltd				
High Tops plc				
Total				

(c) **Using your answers to (a) and (b), above calculate the cash balance.**

£

(d) **Using your answers to (a) and (b), above calculate the bank balance.**

£

(e) **Will the bank balance calculated in (d) above be a debit or credit balance?**

	✓
Debit	
Credit	

Task 2.2

On 28 June Russell Hardware received the following bank statement as at 23 June.

Far Bank PLC					
100 High Street, Manson, MN3 3KJ					
To: Russell Hardware	Account No 76938472		23 June 20XX		
Statement of Account					
Date	Detail	Paid out	Paid in	Balance	
20XX		£	£	£	
04 June	Balance b/f			3,745	C
04 June	Cheque 109829	4,534		789	D
04 June	Cheque 109830	934		1,723	D
05 June	Cheque 109831	629		2,352	D
06 June	Cheque 109833	1,000		3,352	D
12 June	Bank Giro Credit Vista		2,019	1,333	D
13 June	Cheque 109834	643		1,976	D
13 June	Direct Debit Manson DC	200		2,176	D
20 June	Direct Debit Jaspar	760		2,936	D
23 June	Bank charges	34		2,970	D
23 June	Overdraft fee	50		3,020	D
23 June	Paid in at Far Bank		3,209	189	C
D = Debit C = Credit					

The cash book as at 23 June is shown below.

Cash book

Date 20XX	Details	Bank £	Date 20XX	Cheque number	Details	Bank £
01 June	Balance b/f	3,745	01 June	109829	Walker Ltd	4,534
20 June	Striss Ltd	3,209	01 June	109830	Jobber Dee plc	934
21 June	Ladbrake Ltd	1,729	01 June	109831	Street Fare Ltd	629
22 June	Crubbs & Co	3,222	01 June	109832	Urban Mass Ltd	562
	▼		02 June	109833	Ostley Ltd	1,000
	▼		02 June	109834	Quister plc	643
	▼		13 June	109835	Green Grass Ltd	98
	▼		20 June		Jaspar Properties	760
	▼				▼	
	▼				▼	
	▼				▼	
	▼				▼	
	▼				▼	

(a) **Check the items on the bank statement against the items in the cash book.**

(b) **Enter any items in the cash book as needed.**

(c) **Total the cash book and clearly show the balance carried down at 23 June (closing balance) and brought down at 24 June (opening balance).**

(d) **Complete the bank reconciliation statement as at 23 June.**

Bank reconciliation statement as at 23 June 20XX

Balance per bank statement			£	
Add:				
Name:		▼	£	
Name:		▼	£	
Total to add			£	
Less:				
Name:		▼	£	
Name:		▼	£	
Total to subtract			£	
Balance as per cash book			£	

Picklist for line items:

Balance b/d
Balance c/d
Bank charges
Crubbs & Co
Green Grass Ltd
Jaspar Properties
Jobber Dee plc
Ladbrake Ltd
Manson DC
Ostley Ltd
Overdraft fee
Quister plc
Street Fare Ltd
Striss Ltd
Urban Mass Ltd
Vista plc
Walker Ltd

Task 2.3

This is a summary of petty cash payments made by Russell Hardware.

Office Supplies Ltd paid	£26.00 (plus VAT)
Post Office paid	£12.00 (no VAT)
RN Travel paid	£33.00 (no VAT)

(a) **Enter the above transactions, in the order in which they are shown, in the petty cash book.**

(b) **Total the petty cash book and show the balance carried down.**

Petty cash book

Debit side		Credit side					
Details	Amount £	Details	Amount £	VAT £	Postage £	Travel £	Office expenses £
Balance b/f	250.00	▼					
		▼					
		▼					
		▼					
		▼					

Picklist for line items:

Amount
Balance b/d
Balance c/d
Details
Postage
Post Office
Office expenses
Office Supplies Ltd
RN Travel
Travel
VAT

....

Task 2.4

Two amounts have been paid from petty cash:

- Printer paper for £21.60 including VAT
- Courier fee for £28.00 plus VAT

(a) **Complete the petty cash vouchers below.**

Petty cash voucher		
Date: 7.07.XX		
Number: PC567		
10 reams printer paper		
Net	£	
VAT	£	
Gross	£	

Petty cash voucher		
Date: 7.07.XX		
Number: PC568		
Fee to same day courier		
Net	£	
VAT	£	
Gross	£	

Part way through the month the petty cash account had a balance of £98.40. The cash in the petty cash box was checked and the following notes and coins were there.

Notes and coins	£
3 × £20 notes	60.00
1 × £10 note	10.00
1 × £5 note	5.00
13 × £1 coins	13.00
5 × 50p coins	2.50
21 × 10p coins	2.10
12 × 5p coins	0.60

(b) **Reconcile the cash amount in the petty cash box with the balance on the petty cash account.**

Amount in petty cash box	£	
Balance on petty cash account	£	
Difference	£	

At the end of the month the cash in the petty cash box was £11.95.

(c) **Complete the petty cash reimbursement document below to restore the imprest amount of £250.**

Petty cash reimbursement		
Date: 31.07.20XX		
Amount required to restore the cash in the petty cash box	£	

Task 2.5

This is a summary of transactions with customers during the month of June.

(a) **Show whether each entry will be a debit or credit in the sales ledger control account in the general ledger.**

Details	Amount £	Debit ✓	Credit ✓
Balance of trade receivables at 1 June	10,298		
Goods sold on credit	13,289		
Payments received from credit customers	15,296		
Discounts allowed	425		
Goods returned by credit customers	1,046		

(b) **What will be the balance brought down on 1 July on the above account?**

	✓
Debit £6,820	
Credit £6,820	
Debit £9,762	
Credit £9,762	
Debit £10,834	
Credit £10,834	

The following debit balances were in the sales ledger on 1 July.

	£
Kendrick plc	928
Askwith Ltd	102
Raston Permanent Ltd	1,652
Biomass plc	73
Nistral plc	2,009
Larkmead & Co	1,999

(c) **Reconcile the balances shown above with the sales ledger control account balance you have calculated in part (b).**

	£
Sales ledger control account balance as at 30 June	
Total of sales ledger accounts as at 30 June	
Difference	

(d) **What may have caused the difference you calculated in part (c)?**

	✓
Goods returned may have been omitted from the sales ledger	
Discounts allowed may have been omitted from the sales ledger	
Goods returned may have been entered in the sales ledger twice	
Sales invoices may have been entered in the sales ledger twice	

It is important to reconcile the sales ledger control account on a regular basis.

(e) **Which of the following statements is True?**

	✓
Reconciliation of the sales ledger control account assures managers that the amount showing as outstanding from customers is correct	
Reconciliation of the sales ledger control account assures managers that the amount showing as outstanding to suppliers is correct	
Reconciliation of the sales ledger control account will show if a purchases invoice has been omitted from the purchases ledger	
Reconciliation of the sales ledger control account will show if a sales invoice has been omitted from the purchases ledger	

Task 2.6

The following is an extract from Russell Hardware's books of prime entry.

Totals for quarter		
Sales day book		**Purchases day book**
Net: £18,725		Net: £11,025
VAT: £3,745		VAT: £2,205
Gross: £22,470		Gross: £13,230
Sales returns day book		**Purchases returns day book**
Net: £1,925		Net: £700
VAT: £385		VAT: £140
Gross: £2,310		Gross: £840
Cash book		
Net cash sales: £350		
VAT: £70		
Gross cash sales: £420		

(a) **What will be the entries in the VAT control account to record the VAT transactions in the quarter?**

VAT control

Details	Amount £	Details	Amount £
▼		▼	
▼		▼	
▼		▼	
▼		▼	
▼		▼	
▼		▼	

Picklist for line items:

Cash book
Cash sales
Purchases
Purchases day book
Purchases returns
Purchases returns day book
Sales
Sales day book
Sales returns
Sales returns day book
VAT

The VAT return has been completed and shows an amount owing to HM Revenue and Customs of £1,365.

(b) **Is the VAT return correct?**

	✓
Yes	
No	

Task 2.7

(a) **From the list below identify TWO methods of making a non-automated payment.**

Service	Method of making non-automated payment? ✓
Cheque	
BACS	
Cash	
Direct debit	
CHAPS	

(b) **Show whether each of the following statements about banking services is True or False.**

	True ✓	False ✓
A customer with a current account at a bank will usually be able to operate it with a debit card		
An overdraft is an arrangement whereby the customer can withdraw more money from the account than they have in it up to a certain limit		
A dishonoured cheque is sent back to the payee's bank so that the payee can pursue payment in some other way		
A cheque drawn on Bank A and paid in at Bank B will normally take four days to be paid		
A customer with a credit balance on its cash book must have a bank statement that shows a credit balance		
An aged trade receivables analysis will assist a business when reconciling its bank statement to its cash book		

Task 2.8

Russell Hardware receives payment from customers and makes payments to suppliers in a variety of ways.

(a) **Select THREE checks that have to be made on the payment method shown below when received from customers.**

Checks to be made	Telephone debit card payment ✓
Check expiry date	
Check issue number	
Check not post dated	
Check security number	
Check words and figures match	
Check card has not been tampered with	

(b) **Show whether each of the statements below is True or False.**

	True ✓	False ✓
When Russell Hardware makes a payment to a supplier by cheque, the amount leaves the business's bank current account immediately the supplier receives the cheque		
When Russell Hardware makes a payment to a supplier by credit card, the amount paid does not affect the bank current account		
When Russell Hardware makes a payment to a supplier by debit card, a charge for this service is always made by the supplier's bank to Russell Hardware		

BPP PRACTICE ASSESSMENT 1
BASIC ACCOUNTING II

ANSWERS

Basic Accounting II BPP practice assessment 1

Section 1

Task 1.1

(a)

Account name	Amount £	Debit ✓	Credit ✓
Suspense	2,436		✓

(b)

Error in the general ledger	Error disclosed by the trial balance ✓	Error NOT disclosed by the trial balance ✓
Writing in the balance on the office stationery account incorrectly	✓	
Recording a purchase from a credit supplier for £5,000 (no VAT) as £500 in both the purchases and the purchases ledger control accounts		✓
Recording a receipt from a credit customer in the cash sales account		✓
Recording a credit note from a supplier on the debit side of the purchases ledger control account and the debit side of the purchases returns account	✓	
Recording a bank receipt from a customer on the credit side of both the bank and the sales ledger control account	✓	
Recording a receipt from a credit customer in the bank account and sales ledger control account only		✓

Task 1.2

(a)

Account name	Amount £	Debit	Credit
Irrecoverable debts	1,120	✓	
VAT	224	✓	
Sales ledger control	1,344		✓

(b)

Account name	Amount £	Debit ✓	Credit ✓
Capital	10,000		✓
Cash at bank	2,500	✓	
Computer	750	✓	
Furniture and fittings	950	✓	
Heat and light	100	✓	
Loan from bank	5,000		✓
Office expenses	320	✓	
Petty cash	200	✓	
Purchases	9,680	✓	
Rent and rates	500	✓	
Journal to record the opening entries of new business			

Task 1.3

(a) Record the wages expense

Account name	Amount £	Debit ✓	Credit ✓
Wages expense	8,259	✓	
Wages control	8,259		✓

(b) Record the HM Revenue and Customs liability

Account name	Amount £	Debit ✓	Credit ✓
Wages control	2,695	✓	
HM Revenue and Customs	2,695		✓

(c) Record the net wages paid to the employees

Account name	Amount £	Debit ✓	Credit ✓
Wages control	5,474	✓	
Bank	5,474		✓

(d) Record the pension administrator liability

Account name	Amount £	Debit ✓	Credit ✓
Wages control	90	✓	
Pension administrator	90		✓

Task 1.4

(a)

(i) Remove the incorrect entry

Account name	Amount £	Debit ✓	Credit ✓
Purchases ledger control	8,844	✓	

(ii) Record the correct entry

Account name	Amount £	Debit ✓	Credit ✓
Purchases ledger control	8,448		✓

(iii) Remove the suspense account balance

Account name	Amount £	Debit ✓	Credit ✓
Suspense	396		✓

(b)

   (i)   Remove the incorrect entries

Account name	Amount £	Debit ✓	Credit ✓
Bank	1,400	✓	
Sales ledger control	1,400		✓

   (ii)   Record the correct entries

Account name	Amount £	Debit ✓	Credit ✓
Bank	1,400	✓	
Sales ledger control	1,400		✓

Task 1.5

Irrecoverable debts

Details	Amount £	Details	Amount £
Suspense	73		

Heat and light

Details	Amount £	Details	Amount £
Office expenses	150		

Marketing expenses

Details	Amount £	Details	Amount £
		Suspense	201

Office expenses

Details	Amount £	Details	Amount £
		Heat and light	150

Suspense

Details	Amount £	Details	Amount £
Marketing expenses	201	Balance b/f	128
		Irrecoverable debts	73

Task 1.6

	Balances extracted on 30 June £	Balances at 1 July	
		Debit £	Credit £
Motor vehicles	13,920	13,920	
Furniture and fittings	9,208	9,208	
Inventory	10,129	10,129	
Cash at bank	673	673	
Petty cash	250	250	
Sales ledger control	7,832	7,832	
Purchases ledger control	4,292		5,306
VAT owing to HM Revenue and Customs	1,029		1,029
Capital	10,000		10,000
Sales	89,125		89,125
Purchases	35,268	35,268	
Purchases returns	1,092		1,092
Wages	18,279	18,279	
Marketing expenses	1,290	1,290	
Office expenses	3,287	3,287	
Rent and rates	2,819	2,819	
Heat and light	1,056	1,650	
Irrecoverable debts	127	127	
Motor expenses	1,820	1,820	
Suspense (credit balance)	420		
Totals		**106,552**	**106,552**

Section 2

Task 2.1

(a)

Cash book – credit side

Details	Discount £	Cash £	Bank £	VAT £	Purchases ledger £	Cash purchases £	Stationery £
Balance b/f			135				
Cranula Ltd		48		8		40	
Gesteor & Co		288		48		240	
S Ransome		167				167	
Weston Ltd	30		1,452		1,452		
Stationery Shop Ltd			240	40			200
Total	30	503	1,827	96	1,452	447	200

(b)

Cash book – debit side

Details	Discount £	Cash £	Bank £	Sales ledger £
Balance b/f		629		
Middle Firth Ltd			673	673
High Tops plc	50		1,092	1,092
Total	50	629	1,765	1,765

(c) The correct answer is: £126 (629 – 503 = 126)

(d) The correct answer is: £62 (1,765 – 1,827)

(e) The correct answer is: Credit

Task 2.2

(a) – (c)

Cash book

Date 20XX	Details	Bank £	Date 20XX	Cheque number	Details	Bank £
01 June	Balance b/f	3,745	01 June	109829	Walker Ltd	4,534
20 June	Striss Ltd	3,209	01 June	109830	Jobber Dee plc	934
21 June	Ladbrake Ltd	1,729	01 June	109831	Street Fare Ltd	629
22 June	Crubbs & Co	3,222	01 June	109832	Urban Mass Ltd	562
12 June	Vista plc	2,019	02 June	109833	Ostley Ltd	1,000
			02 June	109834	Quister plc	643
			13 June	109835	Green Grass Ltd	98
			20 June		Jaspar Properties	760
			13 June		Manson DC	200
			23 June		Bank charges	34
			23 June		Overdraft fee	50
			23 June		Balance c/d	4,480
		13,924				13,924
24 June	Balance b/d	4,480				

(d)

Bank reconciliation statement as at 23 June 20XX

Balance per bank statement		£	189
Add:			
Name:	Ladbrake Ltd	£	1,729
Name:	Crubbs & Co	£	3,222
Total to add		£	4,951
Less:			
Name:	Urban Mass Ltd	£	562
Name:	Green Grass Ltd	£	98
Total to subtract		£	660
Balance as per cash book		£	4,480

Task 2.3

(a) – (b)

Petty cash book

Debit side		Credit side					
Details	Amount £	Details	Amount £	VAT £	Postage £	Travel £	Office expenses £
Balance b/f	250.00	Office Supplies Ltd	31.20	5.20			26.00
		Post Office	12.00		12.00		
		RN Travel	33.00			33.00	
		Balance c/d	173.80				
	250.00		250.00	5.20	12.00	33.00	26.00

Task 2.4

(a)

Petty cash voucher		
Date: 7.07.XX		
Number: PC567		
10 reams printer paper		
Net	£	18.00
VAT	£	3.60
Gross	£	21.60

Petty cash voucher		
Date: 7.07.XX		
Number: PC568		
Fee to same day courier		
Net	£	28.00
VAT	£	5.60
Gross	£	33.60

(b)

Amount in petty cash box	£	93.20
Balance on petty cash account	£	98.40
Difference	£	5.20

(c)

Petty cash reimbursement		
Date: 31.07.20XX		
Amount required to restore the cash in the petty cash box	£	238.05

Task 2.5

(a)

Details	Amount £	Debit ✓	Credit ✓
Balance of receivables at 1 June	10,298	✓	
Goods sold on credit	13,289	✓	
Payments received from credit customers	15,296		✓
Discounts allowed	425		✓
Goods returned by credit customers	1,046		✓

(b) The correct answer is: Debit £6,820

(c)

	£
Sales ledger control account balance as at 30 June	6,820
Total of sales ledger accounts as at 30 June	6,763
Difference	57

(d) The correct answer is: Goods returned may have been entered in the sales ledger twice

(e) The correct answer is: Reconciliation of the sales ledger control account assures managers that the amount showing as outstanding from customers is correct

....

Task 2.6

(a)

VAT control

Details	Amount £	Details	Amount £
Sales returns	385	Sales	3,745
Purchases	2,205	Purchases returns	140
		Cash sales	70

(b) The correct answer is: Yes

....

Task 2.7

(a) The correct answers are: Cheque and Cash

(b)

	True ✓	False ✓
A customer with a current account at a bank will usually be able to operate it with a debit card	✓	
An overdraft is an arrangement whereby the customer can withdraw more money from the account than he has in it up to a certain limit	✓	
A dishonoured cheque is sent back to the payee's bank so that the payee can pursue payment in some other way	✓	
A cheque drawn on Bank A and paid in at Bank B will normally take four days to be paid		✓
A customer with a credit balance on its cash book must have a bank statement that shows a credit balance		✓
An aged trade receivables analysis will assist a business when reconciling its bank statement to its cash book		✓

Task 2.8

(a)

Checks to be made	Telephone debit card payment ✓
Check expiry date	✓
Check issue number	✓
Check not post dated	
Check security number	✓
Check words and figures match	
Check card has not been tampered with	

(b)

	True ✓	False ✓
When Russell Hardware makes a payment to a supplier by cheque, the amount leaves the business's bank current account immediately the supplier receives the cheque		✓
When Russell Hardware makes a payment to a supplier by credit card, the amount paid does not affect the bank current account	✓	
When Russell Hardware makes a payment to a supplier by debit card, a charge for this service is always made by the supplier's bank to Russell Hardware		✓

BPP PRACTICE ASSESSMENT 2
BASIC ACCOUNTING II

Time allowed: 2 hours

Basic Accounting II BPP practice assessment 2

Section 1

Task 1.1

Finn Clothing's trial balance was extracted and did not balance. The debit column of the trial balance totalled £326,537 and the credit column totalled £329,620.

(a) **What entry would be made in the suspense account to balance the trial balance?**

Account name	Amount £	Debit ✓	Credit ✓
Suspense			

It is important to understand the types of error that are disclosed by the trial balance and those that are not.

(b) **Show which of the errors below are, or are not, disclosed by the trial balance.**

Error in the general ledger	Error disclosed by the trial balance ✓	Error NOT disclosed by the trial balance ✓
Making a transposition error in the debit entry from the journal in the general ledger but not in the credit entry		
Recording a sale to a customer for £75 cash (no VAT) as £57 in both the cash account and the sales account		
Recording a payment for a cash purchase (no VAT) in the purchases ledger column of the cash book		
Recording discount allowed to a customer on the debit side of the discount allowed account and the debit side of the sales ledger control account		
Recording a payment to a supplier on the credit side of the supplier's purchases ledger account		
Recording a sales return by debiting the sales ledger control account and crediting the sales returns account		

Task 1.2

A credit customer, Gridhaul Ltd, has ceased trading, owing Finn Clothing £760 plus VAT.

(a) **Record the journal entries needed in the general ledger to write off the net amount and the VAT.**

Account name		Amount £	Debit ✓	Credit ✓
	▼			
	▼			
	▼			

Picklist for line items:

Irrecoverable debts
Gridhaul Ltd
Finn Clothing
Purchases
Purchases ledger control
Sales
Sales ledger control
VAT

(b) Finn Clothing has started a new business, Finn Footware, and a new set of accounts is to be opened. A partially completed journal to record the opening balances is shown below.

Record the journal entries needed in the accounts in the general ledger of Finn Footware to deal with the opening balances.

Account name	Amount £	Debit ✓	Credit ✓
Capital	9,000		
Cash at bank	850		
Furniture and fittings	1,680		
Loan from bank	4,500		
Marketing expenses	300		
Motor expenses	90		
Motor van	1,150		
Purchases	8,200		
Rent and rates	510		
Wages	720		
Journal to record the opening entries of new business			

Task 1.3

Finn Clothing pays its employees by cheque every month and maintains a wages control account. A summary of last month's payroll transactions is shown below:

Item	£
Gross wages	10,267
Employees' NI	716
Income tax	1,540
Employer's pension contributions	150
Employer's NI	1,182

Record the journal entries needed in the general ledger to:

(a) **Record the wages expense**

Account name	Amount £	Debit ✓	Credit ✓
▼			
▼			

(b) **Record the HM Revenue and Customs liability**

Account name	Amount £	Debit ✓	Credit ✓
▼			
▼			

(c) **Record the net wages paid to the employees**

Account name	Amount £	Debit ✓	Credit ✓
▼			
▼			

(d) Record the pension administrator liability

Account name	Amount £	Debit ✓	Credit ✓
▼			
▼			

Picklist for line items:

Bank
Employees' NI
Employer's NI
HM Revenue and Customs
Income tax
Net wages
Pension administrator
Wages control
Wages expense

Task 1.4

Finn Clothing's initial trial balance includes a suspense account with a balance of £1,000.

The error has been traced to the sales day book shown below.

Sales day book

Date 20XX	Details	Invoice number	Total £	VAT £	Net £
30 Jun	Idris plc	5264	1,008	168	840
30 Jun	Venitian Trading	5265	1,824	304	1,520
30 Jun	Slippers & Co	5266	2,592	432	2,160
	Totals		5,424	904	3,520

(a) Identify the error and record the journal entries needed in the general ledger to

   (i) Remove the incorrect entry

Account name	Amount £	Debit ✓	Credit ✓
▼			

(ii) **Record the correct entry**

Account name	Amount £	Debit ✓	Credit ✓
▼			

(iii) **Remove the suspense account balance**

Account name	Amount £	Debit ✓	Credit ✓
▼			

Picklist for line items:

Idris plc
Venitian Trading
Slippers & Co
Purchases
Purchases day book
Purchases ledger control
Purchases returns
Purchases returns day book
Sales
Sales day book
Sales ledger control
Sales returns
Sales returns day book
Suspense
VAT

The entry to record discounts received of £82 from a credit supplier has been recorded as £28.

(b) **Record the journal entries needed in the general ledger to**

(i) **Remove the incorrect entries**

Account name	Amount £	Debit ✓	Credit ✓
▼			
▼			

(ii) **Record the correct entries**

Account name	Amount £	Debit ✓	Credit ✓
▼			
▼			

Picklist for line items:

Bank
Cash
Discounts received
Purchases
Purchases ledger control
Sales
Sales ledger control
Suspense
VAT

Task 1.5

Finn Clothing's trial balance included a suspense account. All the bookkeeping errors have now been traced and the journal entries shown below have been recorded.

Journal entries

Account name	Debit £	Credit £
Suspense	3,000	
Loan		3,000
Administration expenses	265	
Irrecoverable debts		265
Purchases ledger control	174	
Suspense		174

Post the journal entries to the general ledger accounts. Dates are not required.

Administration expenses

Details	Amount £	Details	Amount £
▼			
▼			
▼			

Irrecoverable debts

Details		Amount £	Details	Amount £
	▼			
	▼			
	▼			

Loan

Details		Amount £	Details	Amount £
	▼			
	▼			
	▼			

Purchases ledger control

Details		Amount £	Details	Amount £
	▼			
	▼			
	▼			

Suspense

Details		Amount £	Details	Amount £
	▼		Balance b/f	2,826
	▼			
	▼			

Picklist for line items:

Balance b/d
Administration expenses
Irrecoverable debts
Loan
Purchases ledger control
Suspense

Task 1.6

On 30 June Finn Clothing extracted an initial trial balance which did not balance, and a suspense account was opened. On 1 July journal entries were prepared to correct the errors that had been found, and clear the suspense account. The list of balances in the initial trial balance, and the journal entries to correct the errors, are shown below. The journal entries have not yet been made in the ledger accounts.

Taking into account the journal entries, which will clear the suspense account, re-draft the trial balance by placing the figures in the debit or credit column.

	Balances extracted on 30 June £	Balances at 1 July	
		Debit £	Credit £
Machinery	15,240		
Furniture and fittings	8,690		
Inventory	11,765		
Cash at bank (overdraft)	5,127		
Petty cash	100		
Sales ledger control	72,536		
Purchases ledger control	11,928		
VAT owing to HM Revenue and Customs	2,094		
Capital	80,000		
Sales	98,162		
Purchases	39,278		
Purchases returns	4,120		
Wages	22,855		
Sales returns	110		
Administration expenses	10,287		
Rent and rates	12,745		
Marketing expenses	3,289		
Irrecoverable debts	1,275		
Maintenance	1,571		
Suspense account (debit balance)	1,690		
Totals			

Journal entries

Account name	Debit £	Credit £
Furniture and fittings		8,690
Suspense	8,690	
Furniture and fittings	9,680	
Suspense		9,680

Account name	Debit £	Credit £
Sales returns	350	
Suspense		350
Sales returns	350	
Suspense		350

Section 2

Task 2.1

Finn Clothing has made five payments which are to be entered in its cash book.

Receipts for payments

Received cash with thanks for goods bought. From Finn Clothing, a customer without a credit account. Net £920 VAT £184 Total £1,104 *Wisper & Co*	Received cash with thanks for goods bought. From Finn Clothing, a customer without a credit account. Net £160 VAT £32 Total £192 *Forback Ltd*	Received cash with thanks for goods bought. From Finn Clothing, a customer without a credit account. Net £193 (No VAT) *Cresswell plc*

Cheque book counterfoils

Lampetus Ltd (Purchases ledger account LAM001) £2,135 (Note: Have taken £25 settlement discount) 003456	GMG Maintenance Services (We have no credit account with this supplier) £426 including VAT 003457

(a) **Enter the details from the three receipts and two cheque book stubs into the credit side of the cash book shown below and total each column.**

Cash book – credit side

Details	Discount £	Cash £	Bank £	VAT £	Purchases ledger £	Cash purchases £	Maintenance £
Balance b/f			1,902				
Wisper & Co							
Forback Ltd							
Cresswell plc							
Lampetus Ltd							
GMG Maintenance Services							
Total							

There are also two cheques from credit customers to be entered in Finn Clothing's cash book:

Prickles & Co £2,837
Dreston Proops £3,299 (this customer has taken a £75 discount)

(b) **Enter the above details into the debit side of the cash book and total each column.**

Cash book – debit side

Details	Discount £	Cash £	Bank £	Sales ledger £
Balance b/f		1,593		
Prickles & Co				
Dreston Proops				
Total				

(c) **Using your answers to (a) and (b) above, calculate the cash balance.**

£ [   ]

(d) **Using your answers to (a) and (b) above, calculate the bank balance.**

£ [   ]

(e) Will the bank balance calculated in (d) above be a debit or credit balance?

	✓
Debit	
Credit	

Task 2.2

On 28 June Finn Clothing received the following bank statement as at 23 June.

Rover Bank PLC

32 Main Square, Gridford GR3 1FP

To: Finn Clothing   Account No 33823981   23 June 20XX

Statement of Account

Date	Detail	Paid out	Paid in	Balance
20XX		£	£	£
04 June	Balance b/f			4,278
04 June	Cheque 003912	1,290		2,988
04 June	Cheque 003913	832		2,156
05 June	Cheque 003914	4,435		2,279
06 June	Cheque 003916	378		2,657
12 June	Bank Giro Credit Pebbles Sisters		3,194	537
13 June	Cheque 003917	1,407		870
13 June	Direct debit Business rates	540		1,410
20 June	Direct debit Employer's insurance	261		1,671
23 June	Bank charges	9		1,680
23 June	Overdraft fee	24		1,704
23 June	Paid in at Rover Bank		2,744	1,040

D = Debit C = Credit

The cash book as at 23 June is shown below.

Cash book

Date 20XX	Details	Bank £	Date 20XX	Cheque number	Details	Bank £
01 June	Balance b/f	4,278	01 June	003912	Brisbane plc	1,290
20 June	Faulkners Finery	2,744	01 June	003913	Ventor Ltd	832
21 June	Roustabout plc	2,927	01 June	003914	Strauss Brothers	4,435
22 June	Hampleforth Ltd	456	01 June	003915	Westenholme plc	1,333
		▽	02 June	003916	Ambrosden Hunt Ltd	378
		▽	02 June	003917	Linnie Ltd	1,407
		▽	13 June	003918	Crebber plc	2,366
		▽	20 June		Employer's insurance	261
		▽				▽
		▽				▽
		▽				▽
		▽				▽
		▽				▽
		▽				▽
		▽				▽

(a) **Check the items on the bank statement against the items in the cash book.**

(b) **Enter any items in the cash book as needed.**

(c) **Total the cash book and clearly show the balance carried down at 23 June (closing balance) and brought down at 24 June (opening balance).**

(d) **Complete the bank reconciliation statement as at 23 June.**

Bank reconciliation statement as at 23 June 20XX

Balance per bank statement		£	
Add:			
Name:	▼	£	
Name:	▼	£	
Total to add		£	
Less:			
Name:	▼	£	
Name:	▼	£	
Total to subtract		£	
Balance as per cash book		£	

Picklist for line items:

Balance b/d
Balance c/d
Bank charges
Hampleforth Ltd
Crebber plc
Employer's insurance
Ventor Ltd
Roustabout plc
Business rates
Ambrosden Hunt Ltd
Overdraft fee
Linnie Ltd
Strauss Brothers
Faulkners Finery
Westenholme plc
Pebbles Sisters
Brisbane plc

Task 2.3

This is a summary of petty cash payments made by Finn Clothing.

Quick Bus Company paid	£12.50 (no VAT)
Star's Stationery paid	£18.00 (plus VAT)
Post Office paid	£8.00 (no VAT)

(a) **Enter the above transactions, in the order in which they are shown, in the petty cash book below.**

(b) **Total the petty cash book and show the balance carried down.**

Petty cash book

Debit side		Credit side					
Details	Amount £	Details	Amount £	VAT £	Stationery £	Travel £	Postage £
Balance b/f	120.00	▼					
▼		▼					
▼		▼					
▼		▼					
▼		▼					

Picklist for line items:

Amount
Balance b/d
Balance c/d
Details
Postage
Post Office
Stationery
Star's Stationery
Quick Bus Company
Travel
VAT

Task 2.4

Two amounts have been paid from petty cash:

- Floral display for £36.48 including VAT
- Maintenance for £32.00 plus VAT

(a) **Complete the petty cash vouchers below.**

Petty cash voucher		
Date: 7.07.XX		
Number: PC837		
Floral display for board room		
Net	£	
VAT	£	
Gross	£	

Petty cash voucher		
Date: 7.07.XX		
Number: PC838		
Emergency maintenance service		
Net	£	
VAT	£	
Gross	£	

Part way through the month the petty cash account had a balance of £81.26. The cash in the petty cash box was checked and the following notes and coins were there.

Notes and coins	£
2 × £20 notes	40.00
2 × £10 notes	20.00
2 × £5 notes	10.00
2 × £2 coins	4.00
3 × £1 coins	3.00
1 × 50p coins	0.50
4 × 10p coins	0.40
5 × 5p coins	0.25
19 × 1p coins	0.19

(b) **Reconcile the cash amount in the petty cash box with the balance on the petty cash account.**

Amount in petty cash box	£	
Balance on petty cash account	£	
Difference	£	

At the end of the month the cash in the petty cash box was £7.77.

(c) **Complete the petty cash reimbursement document below to restore the imprest amount of £120.**

Petty cash reimbursement		
Date: 31.07.20XX		
Amount required to restore the cash in the petty cash box	£	

· ·

Task 2.5

This is a summary of transactions with suppliers during the month of June.

(a) **Show whether each entry will be a debit or credit in the purchases ledger control account in the general ledger.**

Details	Amount £	Debit ✓	Credit ✓
Balance of trade payables at 1 June	15,243		
Payments made to credit suppliers	16,297		
Goods purchased on credit	17,209		
Goods returned to credit suppliers	2,187		
Discount received	625		

(b) **What will be the balance brought down on 1 July on the above account?**

	✓
Debit £11,519	
Credit £11,519	
Debit £13,343	
Credit £13,343	
Debit £18,967	
Credit £18,967	

The following credit balances were in the purchases ledger on 1 July.

	£
Rambout plc	1,928
Creakleys	5,326
International Peace Ltd	936
Diamond Lil plc	1,278
Marksman & Co	4,425
Fitzharrys plc	327

(c) **Reconcile the balances shown above with the purchases ledger control account balance you have calculated in part (b).**

	£
Purchases ledger control account balance as at 30 June	
Total of purchases ledger accounts as at 30 June	
Difference	

(d) **What error may have caused the difference you calculated in part (c)?**

	✓
Discounts received may have been omitted from the purchases ledger	
Purchases invoices may have been entered in the purchases ledger control account twice	
Goods returned may have been entered in the purchases ledger twice	
Goods returned may have been omitted from the purchases ledger control account	

It is important to reconcile the purchases ledger control account on a regular basis.

(e) **Which of the following statements is True?**

Reconciliation of the purchases ledger control account	✓
assures managers that the amount showing as outstanding from customers is correct	
assures managers that the amount showing as outstanding to suppliers is correct	
will show if a sales invoice has been omitted from the purchases ledger	
will show if a purchases invoice has been omitted from the sales ledger	

Task 2.6

The following is an extract from Finn Clothing's books of prime entry.

Totals for quarter

Sales day book	**Purchases day book**
Net: £53,550	Net: £16,275
VAT: £10,710	VAT: £3,255
Gross: £64,260	Gross: £19,530
Sales returns day book	**Purchases returns day book**
Net: £2,800	Net: £1,085
VAT: £560	VAT: £217
Gross: £3,360	Gross: £1,302

Cash book
Net cash sales: £840
VAT: £168
Gross cash sales: £1,008

(a) **What will be the entries in the VAT control account to record the VAT transactions in the quarter?**

VAT control

Details		Amount £	Details		Amount £
	▼			▼	
	▼			▼	
	▼			▼	
	▼			▼	
	▼			▼	
	▼			▼	

Picklist for line items:

Cash book
Cash sales
Purchases
Purchases day book
Purchases returns
Purchases returns day book
Sales
Sales day book
Sales returns
Sales returns day book
VAT

The VAT return has been completed and shows an amount owing from HM Revenue and Customs of £7,280.

(b) **Is the VAT return correct?**

	✓
Yes	
No	

Task 2.7

(a) **From the list below identify TWO methods of automated payment.**

Service	Method of making automated payment? ✓
Cheque	
BACS	
Cash	
Standing order	
Interest	

(b) **Show whether the following statements about banking services are True or False.**

	True ✓	False ✓
No entries can be made in a cash book without access to the business's bank statement		
A mortgage is an arrangement whereby the customer can withdraw more money from the account than he has in it up to a certain limit		
A dishonoured cheque is sent back to the drawer's bank so that the drawer can pursue payment in some other way		
A cheque drawn on Bank X and paid in at Bank Y will normally take three days to be paid		
A customer with a current account at a bank will usually be able to operate it with a credit card		
In the absence of timing differences, a customer with a credit balance on its cash book must have a bank statement that shows a debit balance		

Task 2.8

Finn Clothing receives payment from customers in a variety of ways.

(a) **Select TWO checks that should be made on the payment method shown below when received from customers for a cash sale.**

Checks to be made	Cheque payment ✓
Check expiry date	
Check issue number	
Check not post dated	
Check security number	
Check words and figures match	
Check signature to passport	

(b) **Show whether each of the statements below is True or False.**

	True ✓	False ✓
When a customer pays Finn Clothing by cheque, the amount is credited to Finn Clothing's current account immediately it receives the cheque		
When it receives payment from a customer by credit card using an electronic swipe machine, an automated transfer is made into the Finn Clothing's bank current account		
A customer that pays Finn Clothing by standing order makes payment of a regular amount each period		

BPP PRACTICE ASSESSMENT 2
BASIC ACCOUNTING II

ANSWERS

Basic Accounting II BPP practice assessment 2

Section 1

Task 1.1

(a)

Account name	Amount £	Debit ✓	Credit ✓
Suspense	3,083	✓	

(b)

Error in the general ledger	Error disclosed by the trial balance ✓	Error NOT disclosed by the trial balance ✓
Making a transposition error in the debit entry from the journal in the general ledger but not in the credit entry	✓	
Recording a sale to a customer for £75 cash (no VAT) as £57 in both the cash account and the sales account		✓
Recording a payment for a cash purchase (no VAT) in the purchases ledger column of the cash book		✓
Recording discount allowed to a customer on the debit side of the discount allowed account and the debit side of the sales ledger control account	✓	
Recording a payment to a supplier on the credit side of the supplier's purchases ledger account		✓
Recording a sales return by debiting the sales ledger control account and crediting the sales returns account		✓

Task 1.2

(a)

Account name	Amount £	Debit ✓	Credit ✓
Irrecoverable debts	760	✓	
VAT	152	✓	
Sales ledger control	912		✓

(b)

Account name	Amount £	Debit ✓	Credit ✓
Capital	9,000		✓
Cash at bank	850	✓	
Furniture and fittings	1,680	✓	
Loan from bank	4,500		✓
Marketing expenses	300	✓	
Motor expenses	90	✓	
Motor van	1,150	✓	
Purchases	8,200	✓	
Rent and rates	510	✓	
Wages	720	✓	
Journal to record the opening entries of new business			

Task 1.3

(a) Record the wages expense

Account name	Amount £	Debit ✓	Credit ✓
Wages expense	11,599	✓	
Wages control	11,599		✓

(b)   Record the HM Revenue and Customs liability

Account name	Amount £	Debit ✓	Credit ✓
Wages control	3,438	✓	
HM Revenue and Customs	3,438		✓

(c)   Record the net wages paid to the employees

Account name	Amount £	Debit ✓	Credit ✓
Wages control	8,011	✓	
Bank	8,011		✓

(d)   Record the pension administrator liability

Account name	Amount £	Debit ✓	Credit ✓
Wages control	150	✓	
Pension administrator	150		✓

Task 1.4

(a)

(i)   Remove the incorrect entry

Account name	Amount £	Debit ✓	Credit ✓
Sales	3,520	✓	

(ii)   Record the correct entry

Account name	Amount £	Debit ✓	Credit ✓
Sales	4,520		✓

(iii)   Remove the suspense account balance

Account name	Amount £	Debit ✓	Credit ✓
Suspense	1,000	✓	

(b)

(i) Remove the incorrect entries

Account name	Amount £	Debit ✓	Credit ✓
Discounts received	28	✓	
Purchases ledger control	28		✓

(ii) Record the correct entries

Account name	Amount £	Debit ✓	Credit ✓
Discounts received	82		✓
Purchases ledger control	82	✓	

Task 1.5

Administration expenses

Details	Amount £	Details	Amount £
Irrecoverable debts	265		

Irrecoverable debts

Details	Amount £	Details	Amount £
		Administration expenses	265

Loan

Details	Amount £	Details	Amount £
		Suspense	3,000

Purchases ledger control

Details	Amount £	Details	Amount £
Suspense	174		

Suspense

Details	Amount £	Details	Amount £
Loan	3,000	Balance b/f	2,826
		Purchases ledger control	174

Task 1.6

	Balances extracted on 30 June £	Balances at 1 July	
		Debit £	Credit £
Machinery	15,240	15,240	
Furniture and fittings	8,690	9,680	
Inventory	11,765	11,765	
Cash at bank (overdraft)	5,127		5,127
Petty cash	100	100	
Sales ledger control	72,536	72,536	
Purchases ledger control	11,928		11,928
VAT owing to HM Revenue and Customs	2,094		2,094
Capital	80,000		80,000
Sales	98,162		98,162
Purchases	39,278	39,278	
Purchases returns	4,120		4,120
Wages	22,855	22,855	
Sales returns	110	810	
Administration expenses	10,287	10,287	
Rent and rates	12,745	12,745	
Marketing expenses	3,289	3,289	
Irrecoverable debts	1,275	1,275	
Maintenance	1,571	1,571	
Suspense account (debit balance)	1,690		
Totals		201,431	201,431

Section 2

Task 2.1

(a)

Cash book – credit side

Details	Discount £	Cash £	Bank £	VAT £	Purchases ledger £	Cash purchases £	Maintenance £
Balance b/f			1,902				
Wisper & Co		1,104		184		920	
Forback Ltd		192		32		160	
Cresswell plc		193				193	
Lampetus Ltd	25		2,135		2,135		
GMG Maintenance Services			426	71			355
Total	25	1,489	4,463	287	2,135	1,273	355

(b)

Cash book – debit side

Details	Discount £	Cash £	Bank £	Sales ledger £
Balance b/f		1,593		
Prickles & Co			2,837	2,837
Dreston Proops	75		3,299	3,299
Total	75	1,593	6,136	6,136

(c)   The correct answer is: £104 (1,593 – 1,489 = 104)

(d)   The correct answer is: £1,673 (6,136 – 4,463)

(e)   The correct answer is: Debit

Task 2.2

(a) – (c)

Cash book

Date 20XX	Details	Bank £	Date 20XX	Cheque number	Details	Bank £
01 June	Balance b/f	4,278	01 June	003912	Brisbane plc	1,29
20 June	Faulkners Finery	2,744	01 June	003913	Ventor Ltd	83:
21 June	Roustabout plc	2,927	01 June	003914	Strauss Brothers	4,43
22 June	Hampleforth Ltd	456	01 June	003915	Westenholme plc	1,33
12 June	Pebbles Sisters	3,194	02 June	003916	Ambrosden Hunt Ltd	37
			02 June	003917	Linnie Ltd	1,40
			13 June	003918	Crebber plc	2,36
			20 June		Employer's insurance	26
			13 June		Business rates	54
			23 June		Bank charges	
			23 June		Overdraft fee	2
			23 June		Balance c/d	72
		13,599				13,59
24 June	Balance b/d	724				

(d)

Bank reconciliation statement as at 23 June 20XX

Balance per bank statement		£	1,040
Add:			
Name:	Roustabout plc	£	2,927
Name:	Hampleforth Ltd	£	456
Total to add		£	3,383
Less:			
Name:	Westenholme plc	£	1,333
Name:	Crebber plc	£	2,366
Total to subtract		£	3,699
Balance as per cash book		£	724

Task 2.3

Petty cash book

Debit side		Credit side					
Details	Amount £	Details	Amount £	VAT £	Stationery £	Travel £	Postage £
Balance b/f	120.00	Quick Bus Company	12.50			12.50	
		Star's Stationery	21.60	3.60	18.00		
		Post Office	8.00				8.00
		Balance c/d	77.90				
	120.00		120.00	3.60	18.00	12.50	8.00

Task 2.4

(a)

Petty cash voucher		
Date: 7.07.XX		
Number: PC837		
Floral display for board room		
Net	£	30.40
VAT	£	6.08
Gross	£	36.48

Petty cash voucher		
Date: 7.07.XX		
Number: PC838		
Emergency maintenance service		
Net	£	32.00
VAT	£	6.40
Gross	£	38.40

(b)

Amount in petty cash box	£	78.34
Balance on petty cash account	£	81.26
Difference	£	2.92

(c)

Petty cash reimbursement		
Date: 31.07.20XX		
Amount required to restore the cash in the petty cash box	£	112.23

Task 2.5

(a)

Details	Amount £	Debit ✓	Credit ✓
Balance of trade payables at 1 June	15,243		✓
Payments made to credit suppliers	16,297	✓	
Goods purchased on credit	17,209		✓
Goods returned to credit suppliers	2,187	✓	
Discount received	625	✓	

(b) The correct answer is: Credit £13,343

(c)

	£
Purchases ledger control account balance as at 30 June	13,343
Total of purchases ledger accounts as at 30 June	14,220
Difference	877

(d) The correct answer is: Discounts received may have been omitted from the purchases ledger

(e) The correct answer is: assures managers that the amount showing as outstanding to suppliers is correct

Task 2.6

(a)

VAT control

Details	Amount £	Details	Amount £
Sales returns	560	Sales	10,710
Purchases	3,255	Purchases returns	217
		Cash sales	168

(b) The correct answer is: No

The account has a credit balance of £7,280, that is the business owes HMRC £7,280

....

Task 2.7

(a) The correct answers are: BACS and Standing order

(b)

	True ✓	False ✓
No entries can be made in a cash book without access to the business's bank statement		✓
A mortgage is an arrangement whereby the customer can withdraw more money from the account than he has in it up to a certain limit		✓
A dishonoured cheque is sent back to the drawer's bank so that the drawer can pursue payment in some other way		✓
A cheque drawn on Bank X and paid in at Bank Y will normally take three days to be paid	✓	
A customer with a current account at a bank will usually be able to operate it with a credit card		✓
In the absence of timing differences, a customer with a credit balance on its cash book must have a bank statement that shows a debit balance	✓	

....

Task 2.8

(a) The correct answers are: Check not post dated and Check words and figures match

(b)

	True ✓	False ✓
When a customer pays Finn Clothing by cheque, the amount is credited to Finn Clothing's current account immediately it receives the cheque		✓
When it receives payment from a customer by credit card using an electronic swipe machine, an automated transfer is made into the Finn Clothing's bank current account	✓	
A customer that pays Finn Clothing by standing order makes payment of a regular amount each period	✓	

BPP PRACTICE ASSESSMENT 3
BASIC ACCOUNTING II

Time allowed: 2 hours

Basic Accounting II BPP practice assessment 3

Section 1

Task 1.1

Scriven Trading's trial balance was extracted and did not balance. The debit column of the trial balance totalled £401,845 and the credit column totalled £398,206.

(a) **What entry would be made in the suspense account to balance the trial balance?**

Account name	Amount £	Debit ✓	Credit ✓
Suspense			

It is important to understand the types of error that are disclosed by the trial balance and those that are not.

(b) **Show which of the errors below are, or are not, disclosed by the trial balance.**

Error in the general ledger	Error disclosed by the trial balance ✓	Error NOT disclosed by the trial balance ✓
For a cash sale of £340 (no VAT), recording the amount as £34 in the cash book		
Recording £50 discount received on the credit side of SLCA and the debit side of the discount received account		
Recording a purchase from a supplier for £180 including VAT as £180 in the PLCA and purchases accounts and £30 in the VAT account		
Making a transposition error when transferring a balance from the ledger account to the trial balance		
Recording a payment from a credit customer for £200 in the debit side of the sales ledger account		
Making a casting error in the total column of the sales returns day book		

Task 1.2

A credit customer, Havelock Co, has ceased trading, owing Scriven Trading £1,560 including VAT.

(a) **Record the journal entries needed in the general ledger to write off the net amount and the VAT.**

Account name		Amount £	Debit ✓	Credit ✓
	▼			
	▼			
	▼			

Picklist for line items:

Irrecoverable debts
Havelock Co
Scriven Trading
Purchases
Purchases ledger control
Sales
Sales ledger control
VAT

(b) Scriven Trading has started a new business, Scriven Supplies, and a new set of accounts is to be opened. A partially completed journal to record the opening balances is shown below.

Record the journal entries needed in the accounts in the general ledger of Scriven Supplies to deal with the opening balances.

Account name	Amount £	Debit ✓	Credit ✓
Capital	14,560		
Bank overdraft	2,380		
Computer equipment	12,840		
Loan from bank	8,100		
Administration expenses	790		
Travel expenses	330		
Machinery	9,800		
Purchases	3,250		
Sales	2,370		
Wages	400		
Journal to record the opening entries of new business			

Task 1.3

Scriven Trading pays its employees by cheque every month and maintains a wages control account. A summary of last month's payroll transactions is shown below:

Item	£
Gross wages	15,409
Employees' NI	781
Income tax	1,673
Employees' social club contributions	150
Employer's NI	2,390

Record the journal entries needed in the general ledger to:

(a) **Record the wages expense**

Account name	Amount £	Debit ✓	Credit ✓
▼			
▼			

(b) **Record the HM Revenue and Customs liability**

Account name	Amount £	Debit ✓	Credit ✓
▼			
▼			

(c) **Record the net wages paid to the employees**

Account name	Amount £	Debit ✓	Credit ✓
▼			
▼			

(d) **Record the social club administrator liability**

Account name	Amount £	Debit ✓	Credit ✓
▼			
▼			

Picklist for line items:

Bank
Employees' NI
Employer's NI
HM Revenue and Customs
Income tax
Net wages
Social club administrator
Wages control
Wages expense

Task 1.4

Scriven Trading's initial trial balance includes a suspense account with a balance of £63. The error has been traced to the sales returns day book shown below.

Sales returns day book

Date 20XX	Details	Credit note number	Total £	VAT £	Net £
30 Jun	Humber Ltd	201	3,396	566	2,830
30 Jun	Stomes Co	202	1,848	308	1,540
30 Jun	Carswell Brothers	203	864	144	720
	Totals		6,108	1,081	5,090

(a) **Identify the error and record the journal entries needed in the general ledger to**

(i) **Remove the incorrect entry**

Account name	Amount £	Debit ✓	Credit ✓
▼			

(ii) **Record the correct entry**

Account name	Amount £	Debit ✓	Credit ✓
▼			

(iii) **Remove the suspense account balance**

Account name	Amount £	Debit ✓	Credit ✓
▼			

Picklist for line items:

Carswell Brothers
Humber Ltd
Purchases
Purchases day book
Purchases ledger control
Purchases returns
Purchases returns day book
Sales
Sales day book
Sales ledger control
Sales returns
Sales returns day book
Stomes Co
Suspense
VAT

The entry to record a receipt from a credit customer of £2,309 has been recorded as £2,930.

(b) **Record the journal entries needed in the general ledger to**

(i) **Remove the incorrect entries**

Account name	Amount £	Debit ✓	Credit ✓
▼			
▼			

(ii) **Record the correct entries**

Account name	Amount £	Debit ✓	Credit ✓
▼			
▼			

Picklist for line items:

Bank
Cash
Discounts received
Purchases
Purchases ledger control
Sales
Sales ledger control
Suspense
VAT

Task 1.5

Scriven Trading's trial balance included a suspense account. All the bookkeeping errors have now been traced and the journal entries shown below have been recorded.

Journal entries

Account name	Debit £	Credit £
Sales ledger control	205	
Suspense		205
Irrecoverable debts	189	
Suspense		189
Motor vehicles	3,300	
Machinery		3,300

Post the journal entries to the general ledger accounts. Dates are not required.

Irrecoverable debts

Details	Amount £	Details	Amount £
▼		▼	
▼		▼	
▼		▼	

Machinery

Details	Amount £	Details	Amount £
▼		▼	
▼		▼	
▼		▼	

Motor vehicles

Details	Amount £	Details	Amount £
▼		▼	
▼		▼	
▼		▼	

Sales ledger control

Details		Amount £	Details		Amount £
	▼			▼	
	▼			▼	
	▼			▼	

Suspense

Details		Amount £	Details		Amount £
Balance b/f		394		▼	
	▼			▼	
	▼			▼	

Picklist for line items:

Balance b/d
Irrecoverable debts
Machinery
Motor vehicles
Sales ledger control
Suspense
Empty

Task 1.6

On 30 June Scriven Trading extracted an initial trial balance which did not balance, and a suspense account was opened. On 1 July journal entries were prepared to correct the errors that had been found, and clear the suspense account. The list of balances in the initial trial balance, and the journal entries to correct the errors, are shown below. The journal entries have not yet been made in the ledger accounts.

Taking into account the journal entries, which will clear the suspense account, re-draft the trial balance by placing the figures in the debit or credit column.

	Balances extracted on 30 June £	Balances at 1 July	
		Debit £	Credit £
Motor vehicles	12,300		
Machinery	17,650		
Inventory	4,380		
Cash at bank	1,470		
Petty cash	150		
Sales ledger control	43,330		
Purchases ledger control	9,820		
VAT owing to HM Revenue and Customs	2,660		
Capital	25,000		
Sales	173,200		
Purchases	79,610		
Purchases returns	1,640		
Wages	40,650		
Sales returns	2,170		
Office expenses	1,260		
Bank loan	14,390		
Production expenses	16,240		
Irrecoverable debts	2,880		
Travel expenses	1,960		
Suspense account (debit balance)	2,660		
Totals			

Journal entries

Account name	Debit £	Credit £
Purchases ledger control	9,820	
Suspense		9,820
Purchases ledger control		9,280
Suspense	9,280	

Account name	Debit £	Credit £
Office expenses	1,060	
Suspense		1,060
Office expenses	1,060	
Suspense		1,060

Section 2

Task 2.1

Scriven Trading has made five payments which are to be entered in its cash book.

Receipts for payments

Received cash with thanks for goods bought.	Received cash with thanks for goods bought.	Received cash with thanks for goods bought.
From Scriven Trading, a customer without a credit account.	From Scriven Trading, a customer without a credit account.	From Scriven Trading, a customer without a credit account.
Net £640 VAT £128 Total £768	Net £265 VAT £53 Total £318	Net £501 (No VAT)
Amdegus Ltd	*Strenta Co*	*Banrix & Sons*

Cheque book counterfoils

Diston Ltd (Purchases ledger account DIS057) £4,295 (Note: Have taken £33 settlement discount) 209345	Opra Office Supplies (We have no credit account with this supplier) £336 including VAT 209346

(a) **Enter the details from the three receipts and two cheque book stubs into the credit side of the cash book shown below and total each column.**

Cash book – credit side

Details	Discount £	Cash £	Bank £	VAT £	Purchases ledger £	Cash purchases £	Office expenses £
Balance b/f			1,249				
Amdegus Ltd							
Strenta Co							
Banrix & Sons							
Diston Ltd							
Opra Office Supplies							
Total							

There are also two cheques from credit customers to be entered in Scriven Trading's cash book:

Vampeter Ltd £1,256
Propos Co £8,903 (this customer has taken a £100 discount)

(b) **Enter the above details into the debit side of the cash book and total each column.**

Cash book – debit side

Details	Discount £	Cash £	Bank £	Sales ledger £
Balance b/f		1,869		
Vampeter Ltd				
Propos Co				
Total				

(c) **Using your answers to (a) and (b) above, calculate the cash balance.**

£ [ ]

(d) **Using your answers to (a) and (b) above, calculate the bank balance.**

£ [ ]

(e) **Will the bank balance calculated in (d) above be a debit or credit balance?**

	✓
Debit	
Credit	

....

Task 2.2

On 28 June Scriven Trading received the following bank statement as at 23 June.

Strongs Bank PLC					
14-18 High Street, Handtown HA3 9XC					
To: Scriven Trading		Account No 11115627		23 June 20XX	
		Statement of Account			
Date	Detail	Paid out	Paid in	Balance	
20XX		£	£	£	
04 June	Balance b/f			1,629	C
04 June	Cheque 112341	782		847	C
04 June	Cheque 112342	1,435		588	D
05 June	Cheque 112343	5,003		5,591	D
06 June	Cheque 112345	909		6,500	D
12 June	Bank Giro Credit Longwall Co		8,014	1,514	C
13 June	Cheque 112346	2,387		873	D
13 June	Direct debit Business rates	470		1,343	D
20 June	Direct debit Trio Rentals	650		1,993	D
23 June	Bank charges (1)	15		2,008	D
23 June	Bank charges (2)	61		2,069	D
23 June	Paid in at Strongs Bank		5,839	3,770	C
D = Debit C = Credit					

The cash book as at 23 June is shown below.

Cash book

Date 20XX	Details	Bank £	Date 20XX	Cheque number	Details	Bank £
01 June	Balance b/f	1,629	01 June	112341	Fieldens & Co	782
20 June	Esterholme plc	5,839	01 June	112342	Quisdem plc	1,435
21 June	Moben Triss	3,279	01 June	112343	Pressway and Sons	5,003
22 June	Stoney Crane	1,207	01 June	112344	Kibble Co	3,226
	▼		02 June	112345	Nimble Partners	909
	▼		02 June	112346	Folly Bridge Ltd	2,387
	▼		13 June	112347	Fosdyke Ltd	846
	▼		20 June		Trio Rentals	650
	▼				▼	
	▼				▼	
	▼				▼	
	▼				▼	
	▼				▼	

(a) **Check the items on the bank statement against the items in the cash book.**

(b) **Enter any items in the cash book as needed.**

(c) **Total the cash book and clearly show the balance carried down at 23 June (closing balance) and brought down at 24 June (opening balance).**

(d) **Complete the bank reconciliation statement as at 23 June.**

Bank reconciliation statement as at 23 June 20XX

Balance per bank statement		£	
Add:			
Name:	▼	£	
Name:	▼	£	
Total to add		£	
Less:			
Name:	▼	£	
Name:	▼	£	
Total to subtract		£	
Balance as per cash book		£	

Picklist for line items:

Balance b/d
Balance c/d
Bank charges (1)
Bank charges (2)
Business rates
Esterholme plc
Fieldens & Co
Folly Bridge Ltd
Fosdyke Ltd
Kibble Co
Longwall Co
Moben Triss
Nimble Partners
Pressway and Sons
Quisdem plc
Stoney Crane
Trio Rentals
Empty

Task 2.3

This is a summary of petty cash payments made by Scriven Trading.

Post office paid	£8.70 (no VAT)
Harry's Cafe paid	£26.30 (no VAT)
Tune Travel paid	£32.40 (plus VAT)

(a) **Enter the above transactions, in the order in which they are shown, in the petty cash book below.**

(b) **Total the petty cash book and show the balance carried down.**

Petty cash book

Debit side		Credit side					
Details	Amount £	Details	Amount £	VAT £	Entertainment £	Travel £	Postage £
Balance b/f	180.00						
		▼					
		▼					
		▼					
		▼					

Picklist for line items:

Amount
Balance b/d
Balance c/d
Details
Entertainment
Harry's Café
Postage
Post Office
Travel
Tune Travel
VAT
Empty

Task 2.4

Two amounts have been paid from petty cash:

- Printer paper for £16.25 plus VAT
- Urgent courier for £41.40 including VAT

(a) **Complete the petty cash vouchers below.**

Petty cash voucher		
Date: 7.07.XX		
Number: PC398		
Printer paper		
Net	£	
VAT	£	
Gross	£	

Petty cash voucher		
Date: 7.07.XX		
Number: PC399		
Urgent courier		
Net	£	
VAT	£	
Gross	£	

Part way through the month the petty cash account had a balance of £73.17. The cash in the petty cash box was checked and the following notes and coins were there.

Notes and coins	£
2 × £20 notes	40.00
2 × £10 notes	20.00
1 × £5 notes	5.00
2 × £2 coins	4.00
2 × £1 coins	2.00
0 × 50p coins	0.00
1 × 10p coins	0.10
1 × 5p coins	0.05
7 × 1p coins	0.07

(b) **Reconcile the cash amount in the petty cash box with the balance on the petty cash account.**

Amount in petty cash box	£	
Balance on petty cash account	£	
Difference	£	

At the end of the month the cash in the petty cash box was £8.53.

(c) **Complete the petty cash reimbursement document below to restore the imprest amount of £180.**

Petty cash reimbursement		
Date: 31.07.20XX		
Amount required to restore the cash in the petty cash box	£	

Task 2.5

This is a summary of transactions with customers during the month of June.

(a) **Show whether each entry will be a debit or credit in the sales ledger control account in the general ledger.**

Details	Amount £	Debit ✓	Credit ✓
Balance of trade receivables at 1 June	13,289		
Payments received from credit customers	14,911		
Goods sold on credit	16,435		
Goods returned by credit customers	1,452		
Discount allowed	43		

(b) **What will be the balance brought down on 1 July on the above account?**

	✓
Debit £16,222	
Credit £16,222	
Debit £13,404	
Credit £13,404	
Debit £13,318	
Credit £13,318	

The following debit balances were in the sales ledger on 1 July.

	£
Sistema plc	2,826
Pardew and Sons	983
Lascelles plc	1,330
Gimsters Co	762
Jerowby Fine	5,111
Masonry Parks	2,360

(c) **Reconcile the balances shown above with the sales ledger control account balance you have calculated in part (b).**

	£
Sales ledger control account balance as at 30 June	
Total of sales ledger accounts as at 30 June	
Difference	

(d) **What error may have caused the difference you calculated in part (c)?**

	✓
Discounts allowed may have been omitted from the control account	
A transposition error in entering an invoice in the sales day book	
An irrecoverable debt write-off omitted from the sales ledger	
A credit note entered twice in the sales ledger	

It is important to reconcile the sales ledger control account on a regular basis.

(e) **Which of the following statements is True?**

Reconciliation of the sales ledger control account	✓
assures managers that the amount showing as cash at bank is correct	
assures managers that the amount showing as outstanding to suppliers is correct	
will show if a sales invoice has been omitted from the sales ledger	
will show if a payment has been omitted from the purchases ledger	

Task 2.6

The following is an extract from Scriven Trading's books of prime entry.

Totals for quarter

Sales day book		Purchases day book	
Net:	£21,430	Net:	£11,720
VAT:	£4,286	VAT:	£2,344
Gross:	£25,716	Gross:	£14,064

Sales returns day book		Purchases returns day book	
Net:	£1,260	Net:	£970
VAT:	£252	VAT:	£194
Gross:	£1,512	Gross:	£1,164

Cash book

Net cash sales:	£1,350
VAT:	£270
Gross cash sales:	£1,620

(a) **What will be the entries in the VAT control account to record the VAT transactions in the quarter?**

VAT control

Details		Amount £	Details		Amount £
	▼			▼	
	▼			▼	
	▼			▼	
	▼			▼	
	▼			▼	
	▼			▼	

Picklist:

Cash book
Cash sales
Purchases
Purchases day book
Purchases returns
Purchases returns day book
Sales
Sales day book
Sales returns
Sales returns day book
VAT
Empty

304

The VAT return has been completed and shows an amount owing to HM Revenue and Customs of £1,641.

(b) **Is the VAT return correct?**

	✓
Yes	
No	

Task 2.7

(a) **From the list below identify TWO methods of automated payment.**

Service	Method of making automated payment? ✓
CHAPS	
Cheque	
Bank draft	
Cash	
BACS	

(b) **Show whether the following statements about banking services are True or False.**

	True ✓	False ✓
A bank's nightsafe allows customers to withdraw cash whenever they wish		
The 'account payee' crossing on a cheque means that it must only be paid into a bank account in the payee's name		
On a bank statement, an overdrawn balance is called a credit balance		
The clearing system for debit card payments means they are taken out of the bank account after three days		
A bank will charge its customer a fee for making a CHAPS payment		
A bank is entitled to debit its customer's overdrawn account with interest due		

Task 2.8

Scriven Trading receives payment from customers in a variety of ways.

(a) **Select TWO checks that should be made on the payment method shown below when received from customers for a cash sale.**

Checks to be made	Cheque payment ✓
Check words and figures match	
Check issue number	
Check signature to driving licence	
Check not post dated	
Check expiry date	
Check security number	

(b) **Show whether each of the statements below is True or False.**

	True ✓	False ✓
When a customer pays Scriven Trading by cheque, the amount is credited to Scriven Trading's current account three working days after presenting the cheque at its bank		
A customer's credit card payment processed using EFTPOS means that Scriven Trading receives the funds on the day of the transaction		
If Scriven Trading wishes to pay irregular amounts at regular times to a supplier it should use a standing order		

BPP PRACTICE ASSESSMENT 3
BASIC ACCOUNTING II

ANSWERS

Basic Accounting II BPP practice assessment 3

Section 1

Task 1.1

(a)

Account name	Amount £	Debit ✓	Credit ✓
Suspense	3,639		✓

(b)

Error in the general ledger	Error disclosed by the trial balance ✓	Error NOT disclosed by the trial balance ✓
For a cash sale of £340 (no VAT), recording the amount as £34 in the cash book		✓
Recording £50 discount received on the credit side of SLCA and the debit side of the discount received account		✓
Recording a purchase from a supplier for £180 including VAT as £180 in the PLCA and purchases accounts and £30 in the VAT account	✓	
Making a transposition error when transferring a balance from the ledger account to the trial balance	✓	
Recording a payment from a credit customer for £200 in the debit side of the sales ledger account		✓
Making a casting error in the total column of the sales returns day book	✓	

Task 1.2

(a)

Account name	Amount £	Debit ✓	Credit ✓
Irrecoverable debts	1,300	✓	
VAT	260	✓	
Sales ledger control	1,560		✓

(b)

Account name	Amount £	Debit ✓	Credit ✓
Capital	14,560		14,560
Bank overdraft	2,380		2,380
Computer equipment	12,840	12,840	
Loan from bank	8,100		8,100
Administration expenses	790	790	
Travel expenses	330	330	
Machinery	9,800	9,800	
Purchases	3,250	3,250	
Sales	2,370		2,370
Wages	400	400	
Journal to record the opening entries of new business			

Task 1.3

(a) Record the wages expense

Account name	Amount £	Debit ✓	Credit ✓
Wages expense	17,799	✓	
Wages control	17,799		✓

(b) Record the HM Revenue and Customs

Account name	Amount £	Debit ✓	Credit ✓
Wages control	4,844	✓	
HM Revenue and Customs	4,844		✓

(c) Record the net wages paid to the employee

Account name	Amount £	Debit ✓	Credit ✓
Wages control	12,805	✓	
Bank	12,805		✓

(d) Record the social club administrator liability

Account name	Amount £	Debit ✓	Credit ✓
Wages control	150	✓	
Social club administrator	150		✓

Task 1.4

(a) (i) Remove the incorrect entry

Account name	Amount £	Debit ✓	Credit ✓
VAT	1,081		✓

(ii) Record the correct entry

Account name	Amount £	Debit ✓	Credit ✓
VAT	1,018	✓	

(iii) Remove the suspense account balance

Account name	Amount £	Debit ✓	Credit ✓
Suspense	63	✓	

(b) (i) Remove the incorrect entries

Account name	Amount £	Debit ✓	Credit ✓
Bank	2,930		✓
Sales ledger control	2,930	✓	

(ii) Record the correct entries

Account name	Amount £	Debit ✓	Credit ✓
Bank	2,309	✓	
Sales ledger control	2,309		✓

Task 1.5

Irrecoverable debts

Details	Amount £	Details	Amount £
Suspense	189		

Machinery

Details	Amount £	Details	Amount £
		Motor vehicles	3,300

Motor vehicles

Details	Amount £	Details	Amount £
Machinery	3,300		

Sales ledger control

Details	Amount £	Details	Amount £
Suspense	205		

Suspense

Details	Amount £	Details	Amount £
Balance b/f	394	Irrecoverable debts	189
		Sales ledger control	205

Task 1.6

	Balances extracted on 30 June £	Balances at 1 July	
		Debit £	Credit £
Motor vehicles	12,300	12,300	
Machinery	17,650	17,650	
Inventory	4,380	4,380	
Cash at bank	1,470	1,470	
Petty cash	150	150	
Sales ledger control	43,330	43,330	
Purchases ledger control	9,820		9,280
VAT owing to HM Revenue and Customs	2,660		2,660
Capital	25,000		25,000
Sales	173,200		173,200
Purchases	79,610	79,610	
Purchases returns	1,640		1,640
Wages	40,650	40,650	
Sales returns	2,170	2,170	
Office expenses	1,260	3,380	
Bank loan	14,390		14,390
Production expenses	16,240	16,240	
Irrecoverable debts	2,880	2,880	
Travel expenses	1,960	1,960	
Suspense account (debit balance)	2,660		
Totals		226,170	226,170

Section 2

Task 2.1

(a) Cash book – credit side

Details	Discount £	Cash £	Bank £	VAT £	Purchases ledger £	Cash purchases £	Office expenses £
Balance b/f			1,249				
Amdegus Ltd		768		128		640	
Strenta Co		318		53		265	
Banrix & Sons		501				501	
Diston Ltd	33		4,295		4,295		
Opra Office Supplies			336	56			280
Total	33	1,587	5,880	237	4,295	1,406	280

(b) Cash book – debit side

Details	Discount £	Cash £	Bank £	Sales ledger £
Balance b/f		1,869		
Vampeter Ltd			1,256	1,256
Propos Co	100		8,903	8,903
Total	100	1,869	10,159	10,159

(c) The correct answer is: £282 (1,869 – 1,587 = 282)

(d) The correct answer is: £4,279 (10,159 – 5,880 = 4,279)

(e) The correct answer is: Debit

....

Task 2.2

Cash book

Date 20XX	Details	Bank £	Date 20XX	Cheque number	Details	Bank £
01 June	Balance b/f	1,629	01 June	112341	Fieldens & Co	782
20 June	Esterholme plc	5,839	01 June	112342	Quisdem plc	1,435
21 June	Moben Triss	3,279	01 June	112343	Pressway and Sons	5,003
22 June	Stoney Crane	1,207	01 June	112344	Kibble Co	3,226
12 June	Longwall Co	8,014	02 June	112345	Nimble Partners	909
			02 June	112346	Folly Bridge Ltd	2,387
			13 June	112347	Fosdyke Ltd	846
			20 June		Trio Rentals	650
			13 June		Business rates	470
			23 June		Bank charges (1)	15
			23 June		Bank charges (2)	61
			23 June		Balance c/d	4,184
		19,968				19,968
24 June	Balance b/d	4,184				

Bank reconciliation statement as at 23 June 20XX

Balance per bank statement		£	3,770
Add:			
Name:	Moben Triss	£	3,279
Name:	Stoney Crane	£	1,207
Total to add		£	4,486
Less:			
Name:	Kibble Co	£	3,226
Name:	Fosdyke Ltd	£	846
Total to subtract		£	4,072
Balance as per cash book		£	4,184

Task 2.3

Petty cash book

Debit side		Credit side					
Details	Amount £	Details	Amount £	VAT £	Entertainment £	Travel £	Postage £
Balance b/f	180.00	Post Office	8.70				8.70
		Harry's Cafe	26.30		26.30		
		Tune Travel	38.88	6.48		32.40	
		Balance c/d	106.12				
	180.00		180.00	6.48	26.30	32.40	8.70

Task 2.4

(a)

Petty cash voucher		
Date: 7.07.XX		
Number: PC398		
Printer paper		
Net	£	16.25
VAT	£	3.25
Gross	£	19.50

Petty cash voucher		
Date: 7.07.XX		
Number: PC399		
Urgent courier		
Net	£	34.50
VAT	£	6.90
Gross	£	41.40

(b)

Amount in petty cash box	£	71.22
Balance on petty cash account	£	73.17
Difference	£	1.95

(c)

Petty cash reimbursement		
Date: 31.07.20XX		
Amount required to restore the cash in the petty cash box	£	171.47

Task 2.5

(a)

Details	Amount £	Debit ✓	Credit ✓
Balance of trade receivables at 1 June	13,289	✓	
Payments received from credit customers	14,911		✓
Goods sold on credit	16,435	✓	
Goods returned by credit customers	1,452		✓
Discount allowed	43		✓

(b) The correct answer is: Debit £13,318

(c)

	£
Sales ledger control account balance as at 30 June	13,318
Total of sales ledger accounts as at 30 June	13,372
Difference	54

(d) The correct answer is: An irrecoverable debt write-off omitted from the sales ledger

(e) The correct answer is: will show if a sales invoice has been omitted from the sales ledger

Task 2.6

(a)

VAT control

Details	Amount £	Details	Amount £
Purchases	2,344	Sales	4,286
Sales returns	252	Purchases returns	194
		Cash sales	270

(b)   The correct answer is: No

Task 2.7

(a)   The correct answers are: CHAPS and BACS

(b)

	True ✓	False ✓
A bank's nightsafe allows customers to withdraw cash whenever they wish		✓
The 'account payee' crossing on a cheque means that it must only be paid into a bank account in the payee's name	✓	
On a bank statement, an overdrawn balance is called a credit balance		✓
The clearing system for debit card payments means they are taken out of the bank account after three days		✓
A bank will charge its customer a fee for making a CHAPS payment	✓	
A bank is entitled to debit its customer's overdrawn account with interest due	✓	

Task 2.8

(a) The correct answers are: Check words and figures match and Check not post dated

(b)

	True ✓	False ✓
When a customer pays Scriven Trading by cheque, the amount is credited to Scriven Trading's current account three working days after presenting the cheque at its bank	✓	
A customer's credit card payment processed using EFTPOS means that Scriven Trading receives the funds on the day of the transaction	✓	
If Scriven Trading wishes to pay irregular amounts at regular times to a supplier it should use a standing order		✓